Stevie Smith's Resistant Antics

Stevie Smith's
Resistant Antics

Laura Severin

THE UNIVERSITY OF WISCONSIN PRESS

The University of Wisconsin Press
114 North Murray Street
Madison, Wisconsin 53715

3 Henrietta Street
London WC2E 8LU, England

1   3   5   4   2

Printed in the United States of America

Excerpt from *Three Guineas* by Virginia Woolf,
copyright © 1938 by Harcourt Brace & Company and
renewed 1966 by Leonard Woolf, reprinted by
permission of the publisher.

Library of Congress Cataloging-in-Publication Data
Severin, Laura, 1958–
Stevie Smith's resistant antics / Laura Severin.
174 pp.   cm.
Includes bibliographical references and index.
ISBN 0-299-15290-1 (cloth: alk. paper).
ISBN 0-299-15294-4 (pbk.: alk. paper).
1. Smith, Stevie, 1902–1971—Criticism and interpretation.
2. Literature and society—England—History—20th century.
3. Women and literature—England—History—20th century.
I. Title.
PR6037.M43Z84   1997
828'.91209—dc20   96-43625

Contents

Acknowledgments

Unlike Stevie, who often saw writing as divesting her of friendships, as when she wrote a good-bye to her "beautiful and lovely friends" at the opening of *Novel on Yellow Paper,* I have found that the writing of this book has only tended to increase my number of lovely, beautiful, and scholarly friends. My first thanks goes to William McBrien and Jack Barbera, Stevie Smith's biographers, who believed in this book when it was only a two-page outline. Mary Braun of the University of Wisconsin Press also supported the book after seeing one, not-too-tidy, chapter. I am indebted again to Jack Barbera, as well as Ann Ardis, for following the book through its many revisions, and to Susan Tarcov for a splendid job of editing. So too am I grateful to Polly Williams and Larry Rudner, colleagues who read this book in a very early draft, and gave me the encouragement I needed to finish. I am only sad that Larry, who died of a brain tumor while the book was in press, will never see it in its finished form; nor will his family—Lauren, Joshua, and Elizabeth—and I have the benefits of his warmth and humor. Thanks also to the librarians at the University of Tulsa, who helped me with the Stevie Smith collection, and to Candice Ward, who gave me the idea of writing a book on Stevie Smith on our long car rides from and to Durham.

And then there are my many British friends who have helped me through the rough spots in writing on so quintessentially British a figure as Stevie Smith. I have been helped frequently by the staffs of the National Sound Archive, the British Library, the Newspaper Library at Colindale, and the BBC Written Archives Centre, but I am especially grateful to Chris Mobbs, who closed down the entire reading room of the National Sound Archive, so that I could sing Stevie Smith's sung poems into a tape recorder, and to David McLachlan, of the British Music Library, who helped me find the very elusive "They played in the beautiful garden." I am also indebted to Penny Summerfield, Alison Light, and Kathleen

Wheeler, who read chapters late in the process and yet nevertheless had a major impact on the final manuscript. Dee Francken gave me a guided tour of North London Collegiate and thus gave me a better idea of the spirit of Stevie Smith's school, even though Smith did not attend the modern campus. Also, a thank you to Peter Dickinson, who not only provided me with invaluable information, but sent me Stevie mementoes as well. And then there is James MacGibbon, Stevie Smith's literary executor, who generously gave me the rights to quote whatever I wanted for this book.

Lastly, to my family, who made me a comfortable Palmer's Green of my own. To my mother, who for some reason always wanted a scholarly daughter, to Edna, who might as well be a sister, and to my husband, Mark Hartley, who was often cook and technical advisor in the same day.

Numerous publishers, particularly those of Stevie Smith's work, have aided this study by allowing me the permission to quote. Stevie Smith's poems and drawings are reprinted by permission of New Directions Publishing Corporation. Stevie Smith: *The Collected Poems of Stevie Smith,* copyright © 1972 by Stevie Smith. Excerpts from Smith's novels, published by Virago, are reprinted by the permission of James MacGibbon. Excerpts from *Me Again: Uncollected Writings of Stevie Smith* by Stevie Smith, edited by Jack Barbera and William McBrien. Copyright © 1981 by James MacGibbon. Reprinted by permission of Farrar, Straus & Giroux, Inc. All other Stevie Smith quotations and drawings copyright © James MacGibbon.

Routledge has allowed me to quote from many volumes: Griselda Pollock's *Vision and Difference: Femininity, Feminism and the Histories of Art,* 1988; Linda Hutcheon's *A Poetics of Postmodernism: History, Theory, Fiction,* 1988; and *The Politics of Postmodernism,* 1989; and Alison Light's *Forever England: Femininity, Literature, and Conservatism between the Wars,* 1991. The following publishers allowed me to reprint from scholarly works: Bay Press (Hal Foster's *The Anti-Aesthetic: Essays on Postmodern Culture,* 1983); The University of Chicago Press (Mitchell's *Iconology: Image, Text, Ideology,* 1986, copyright © 1986 The University of Chicago); W. W. Norton & Company (*Stevie Smith: A Biography* by Frances Spalding. Copyright © 1988 by Frances Spalding. Reprinted by permission of W. W. Norton & Company, Inc.); The University Press of Kentucky (John Snyder's *Prospects of Power: Tragedy, Satire, The Essay,* copyright © 1991 by The University Press of Kentucky, reprinted by permission of the publishers); The University of Nebraska Press (Paul Hernadi's *The Horizon of Literature,* 1982); Macmillan Press Ltd. (Martin Pugh's *Women and the Women's Movement,* 1993); Manchester University Press (C. Geldhill and G. Swanson's *Nationalising Femininity: Culture, Sexuality, and British Cinema in the Second World War,* forth-

Acknowledgments

coming); Methuen and Co. (Toril Moi's *Sexual/Textual Politics*, 1985); Oxford University Press (Kate Whitehead's *The Third Programme: A Literary History*, 1989, by permission of Oxford University Press); Pandora Press (HarperCollins Publishers), Watson, Little Ltd. licensing agents, (Deirdre Beddoe's *Back to Home and Duty: Women between the Wars, 1918–1939*, 1989); Syracuse University Press (Sanford Sternlicht's *In Search of Stevie Smith*, 1991); and Tavistock Publications (Elizabeth Wilson's *Only Halfway to Paradise*, 1980). *Studies in the Novel* permitted quotation of Margaret Stetz's "*The Ghost and Mrs. Muir*: Laughing with the Captain in the House," 28.1 (Spring 1996).

The work has also benefitted from close comparison to those women writers who particularly influenced Smith. Liveright Publishing Corporation provided permission to quote Anita Loos's *Gentlemen Prefer Blondes* and *But Gentlemen Marry Brunettes*, 1983. Rights to quote Dorothy Parker's work were provided by Penguin: "Big Blonde" by Dorothy Parker, copyright 1929, renewed © 1957 by Dorothy Parker; "Glory in the Daytime" by Dorothy Parker, copyright 1933, renewed © 1961 by Dorothy Parker; "Here We Are" by Dorothy Parker, Introduction by Brendan Gill, copyright 1931, renewed © 1959 by Dorothy Parker; "Too Bad" by Dorothy Parker, copyright 1928, renewed © 1956 by Dorothy Parker, from *The Portable Dorothy Parker* by Dorothy Parker, Introduction by Brendan Gill; used by permission of Viking Penguin, a division of Penguin Books USA Inc. Harcourt Brace and Chatto & Windus gave permission to reprint an excerpt from *Three Guineas* by Virginia Woolf.

Stevie Smith's Resistant Antics

1

Introduction

Through Glenda Jackson's much-praised portrayal of Stevie Smith on stage (1977) and screen (1978), the details of the writer's life have become widely known, oftentimes more so than her work as poet, novelist, short story writer, reviewer, and performance artist. Perhaps not surprisingly, this fascination with Smith as a flamboyant character has not been confined to a general audience. In addition to two full-length biographies, Smith's critics have produced numerous published interviews, reminiscences, and biographical readings.[1] This intensely author-centered tradition has led feminist critic Romana Huk to question historical, cultural, and biographical readings, for fear that Smith will continue to be thought of as "the eccentric old British match-up for spinster-poet Emily Dickinson."[2] In an effort to recover Smith's language, Huk argues for an emphasis on close readings of her texts, claiming that "redefining Smith's position of 'ex-centricity' vis-à-vis the traditional heart of her culture" can best be performed through examining the "only world her speakers can know—the text."[3]

Certainly, the emphasis on eccentricity in past readings of women writers has led to their marginalization, but to dismiss historical and cultural readings continues to limit and confine Smith scholarship. As Alison Light cautions, Smith has too often been dismissed as a writer "outside of history."[4] From Smith's biographers, we know her as a witty and caustic individual, but we possess little knowledge of her as a woman writer whose career almost entirely spans a conservative period of backlash against women. There are other worlds—and other texts—by which we can "know" Stevie Smith's work.

A potentially fascinating detail of Smith's life, one that leads from biography to larger cultural concerns, is that she worked most of her life as a secretary for Pearson's (later Newnes, Pearson), one of Britain's main publishers of women's magazines.[5] When she began her job shortly after

3

the conclusion of World War I, the popular media were increasingly clamoring for a return to traditional gender roles, particularly for women.[6] That one of domesticity's sharpest critics should work for a producer of domestic ideology is hardly a coincidence. Smith's diatribes against the women's magazine industry in *Novel on Yellow Paper* (1936) suggest an awareness of the ways in which these magazines' narrative structures and subjects acted, in Rachel DuPlessis's words, as the "working apparatuses of ideology, factories for the 'natural' and 'fantastic' meanings by which we live."[7] Smith's opposition to romantic narratives, with their predictably linear plots, is revealed in her continued suspicion of then-current definitions of love, marriage, and family, as well as her experiments in fractured and/or antilinear art forms. However, drawing a connection between Smith's role in the mass culture industry and her production in the "high" art world challenges many of the received readings of her life and writings, as well as many of the truisms by which literary work has been performed.

THE INTERWAR MASS CULTURE INDUSTRY

Acknowledging that Smith worked in the publishing industry requires fundamentally rethinking her reputation as outsider among her contemporaries. Although Romana Huk has questioned Smith's "eccentrism" within literary tradition, a similar skepticism has yet to be thoroughly applied to her institutional positioning.[8] Smith did possess a network in the industry, though a decidedly female one. Her editorial friends included Narcissa Crowe-Wood (Harriet in *Novel on Yellow Paper*), an editor at Newnes; Kay Dick, first woman director in English publishing and later assistant editor of the Newnes publication *John O'London's Weekly;* and Norah Smallwood, editor and later chairman at Chatto and Windus.[9] In addition, many of Smith's friends were publish[ed] writers. Much has been made of Smith's isolation from other contemporary literary figures, particularly poets, but she knew almost all the leading women novelists of her day: Inez Holden, Olivia Manning, Rosamond Lehmann, Storm Jameson, Rose Macaulay, and Naomi Mitchison.[10] That Smith understood her difficulties in the publishing world in gendered terms, along with those of women friends, is recorded in her letters to Naomi Mitchison.[11]

Through her connection with these women, Smith had a lively understanding of a largely masculinist industry that continued to dictate the tastes of its lowbrow and middlebrow women's readership, while retaining the privilege and power associated with "high" art production. As Andreas Huyssen points out in his influential essay "Mass Culture as Woman," "[the] positioning of woman as avid consumer of pulp . . . also affects the woman writer who has the same kind of ambition as the 'great (male) modernist.'"[12] In order to keep women "in their place" as readers and consumers, where they fuel an extremely profitable industry, it has been historically important to exclude them as producers, either as writers, editors, or publishing participants. Suspicious of all hierarchies, Smith possessed a keen understanding of the financial and psychological underpinnings of the literary hierarchy, as is evidenced by her attacks in *Novel on Yellow Paper,* in poems such as "How far can you Press a Poet?" "Souvenir de Monsieur Poop," "No Categories!" "To School!" "To an American Publisher," "The English," "The Choosers," "The Crown of Gold," and in essays such as the 1958 "History or Poetic Drama?" on T. S. Eliot's *Murder in the Cathedral.*

To suggest that Smith understood the many ways in which the publishing industry can work against women, as both readers and writers, is to challenge another of the truisms by which we have known Smith: that she was hardly a feminist. Ironically, Martin Pumphrey, the first critic to see Smith specifically as a woman writer, has established this case, suggesting that Smith can not be "easily recruited as a feminist."[13] However, his judgment is limited by its ahistoricism and needs to be rethought. Certainly, Smith never accepted or welcomed the label of feminist, but her work needs to be read in light of the period in which she worked, one increasingly conservative with regard to gender roles.

There are many reasons why Smith would have had difficulty self-identifying as a feminist, given her historical positioning. She was only sixteen in 1918, the year some British women over thirty received the vote, and therefore too young to have experienced much of the suffrage movement. As Deirdre Beddoe explains in *Back to Home and Duty,* the suffrage movement had taken sixty years, and many of its leaders were aging Victorians, hardly appealing role models for young girls.[14] Also, as a young woman whose twenties almost exactly coincided with the years in which women under thirty were not allowed to vote (1918–28), Smith would have been politically excluded from the ranks of women who were beginning to exercise their rights.

But most important, Smith seems to have been philosophically at odds with the two definitions of feminism current in the interwar era, both the "old" feminism of women such as Lady Rhondda and Winifred Holtby and the "new" feminism of others such as Eleanor Rathbone, Mary Stocks, and Maude Royden.[15] Although she was closer to the beliefs of the egalitarian "old" feminists, Smith's lower-middle-class background put her at odds with the middle-class and upper-middle-class women whose goal, advancement in the professions, she vaguely saw as self-serving and masculinist. As Deirdre Beddoe attests, women of the lower classes often felt alienated from such individualistic goals.[16] In *Over the Frontier,* Smith caustically dismisses those "pseudo-feminists" who ape masculine behavior, wondering for whose good they work.[17] Her statement on Rebecca West is revealing of Smith's complex and often contradictory beliefs:

I would not call Miss West a feminist, because this suggests—and is meant to— an aggrieved and strident person. I would say, she is on the side of women.[18]

In this passage, Smith reads the label of feminist (as do many women now) as indicating someone who is "aggrieved and strident," i.e., an aggressive individualist who works for her own benefit. But she does admire West for being "on the side of women," which indicates her interest in a definition of feminism that is inclusive, and truly beneficial to women as a group.

Yet if Smith was ambivalent toward "old" feminism, and its class allegiances, she had even less in common with "new" feminists such as Eleanor Rathbone, who believed in women's superiority and uniqueness as a sex. Strongly anti-essentialist, Smith consistently deplored any valorizing of women, as she understood such a move to be a continuation of the Victorian separation of spheres. Her satiric parody of Tennyson's *Maud* in her story "The House of Over-Dew," included in *The Holiday* (1949), shows her to have little patience with the self-sacrificing Victorianism of Mrs. Minnim.[19] Reprinted in Barbera and McBrien's *Me Again,* her reviews "The Better Half?" and "Poems in Petticoats" have been used, as have the comments above, to disprove her interest in feminism.[20] However, they really demonstrate only a Smith uncomfortable with the glorification of women as a group and the machinations of oppositional logic.

In "The Better Half?," a review of a scholarly work on women's history, she wants us to remember that "[w]omen have been good and fought like the devil, but some were bad and loved enclosure. . . ."[21] Fearful that easy valorization of women will not, ultimately, be in their best interests, Smith is not about to participate in reversing hierarchies. Her review of *The Femina Anthology of Poetry,* which she herself contributed to, is skeptical of women's anthologies, but only because she fears the "ancient game" of debates over men and women's collective talents:

Tempted to take a hand in this ancient game, one might try something on these lines: Differences between men and women poets are best seen when the poets are bad. Bad women poets are better characters, they seldom . . . get drunk . . . go to prison . . . shoot the pianist. Their faults are soulfulness and banality. They like to commune (who does not?) with the Deity, Nature, themselves, but the words they use do not quite carry the traffic. Bad men poets are more knowing; often they achieve fame as poets by stopping writing and going on committees. Some bad men poets can persuade people (some people) that tricks and shocks are a substitute for talent. Bad women poets are not so clever about this, STOP, they are not so clever. Of course, good poets of either sex are above these squabbles, at least one hopes they are. Awkward.[22]

In a typical ploy, Smith mimics those who would make sharp distinctions based on sex, revealing that those distinctions ultimately collapse in absurdity.

Neither an egalitarian "old" feminist nor an essentialist "new" feminist, Smith has more in common with later poststructuralist feminists, whom Julia Kristeva names her third generation in "Women's Time." Although Kristeva cautions that her generations of feminism overlap and coexist, she does trace them historically. Kristeva's first generation, which corresponds to the "old" feminism of Smith's period, focused on equality for women. Her second generation, which she ties to "the younger women who came to feminism after May 1968," but which could also be tied to the "new" feminism of Eleanor Rathbone, focused on difference: "Essentially interested in the specificity of female psychology and its symbolic realizations, these women [sought] to give a language to the intrasubjective and corporeal experiences left mute by culture in the past."[23] The third generation, which she sees is "now forming" (in a politically identifiable manner), is concerned with the deconstruction of sexual identity, the "demassification of the problematic of difference."[24] To link Smith with this third generation, those who oppose the rigidity of social constructions of gender, is to see her not as a woman out of time, but as one whose beliefs did not easily match those of other politically recognizable feminist groups of her day.

Though she was unable to label herself a feminist, Smith's views on gender roles are unquestionably radical, given the time period in which she began writing. As historians Cynthia White, Martin Pugh, and Deirdre Beddoe attest, the interwar years mark a return to associations between women and domesticity, to what Martin Pugh calls the "cult of domesticity."[25] According to Deirdre Beddoe, "[t]he single most arresting feature of the interwar years was the strength of the notion that women's place is in the home":

When the First World War ended, women who had contributed so much to the war effort in engineering, on the buses, trams and railways, in the services and in government offices were dismissed in vast numbers and expected to return to the home to fulfil their natural roles as wives, mothers, daughters, and sisters. How quickly praise for our gallant wartime girls gave way to attacks on women who persisted in working or tried to claim dole money! They were dubbed as hussies, pin-money girls, dole scroungers and women who stole men's jobs; by 1920 it was considered wilful and perverse of a woman to wish to earn her own living.[26]

The return to home and hearth was enforced upon women through demobilization policies, restriction of the dole, and marriage bars, but women were coaxed as well as forced. According to Beddoe, "[m]edia images, most notably in the rash of new domestically-orientated women's magazines, put before women the shining ideal of the stay-at-home housewife."[27] These new "domestically-orientated women's magazines" were issued in part by Pearson's, later Newnes, Pearson, Smith's employer. That Smith was familiar with these magazines is made clear by her parodies included in *Novel on Yellow Paper*.

When Smith started working at Pearson's, most likely in 1923, the business of women's magazines was booming. In the interwar years, more than fifty magazines were aimed at women readers.[28] Although these were new publications, the magazines were linked to their Victorian forebears in spreading the message of domesticity to women. Indeed, both Smith's employers, Newnes and Pearson, had inherited their businesses from Victorian fathers.[29] However, the return to the separate-spheres ideal reached a new intensity in the interwar magazine. According to Martin Pugh, "In some degree all of them propagated an ideology of domesticity; perhaps surprisingly some of the new ones did so more blatantly than their older rivals."[30] While Victorian women had taken the separate-spheres concept for granted, perhaps their daughters and granddaughters needed to be more urgently persuaded to take up their traditional roles.

That Pearson's was a major participant in this return to an ideology based on rigid gender differentiation is indicated by the sheer number of magazines they produced. In 1923, Pearson's published three monthlies, *Pearson's Magazine*, *The Royal Magazine* and *The Novel*, as well as five weeklies, *Pearson's Weekly*, *Home Notes*, *Peg's Paper*, *Peg's Companion*, and *Jack's Paper*. For the purpose of this study, *Pearson's Magazine* (1896–1939), *The Royal* (1893–1930), and *Peg's Paper* (1919–40) are the most intriguing, in that they provide a running commentary on women's roles as presented in these forms of mass culture. *Pearson's* and *The Royal* were family magazines, intended to be read by both sexes, but individual stories and articles are very clearly gender-typed: Romances sit next to adventures, beauty tips next to hunting articles. Sex delineation is perhaps more obvious in the magazines intended for working-class audiences, *Peg's Paper* and *Peg's Companion*, where young mill girls are saved by dashing young rescuers, and *Jack's Paper*, where adventurous young men save lost kings or face outlaw Arabian sheiks. Even more than their rivals, Pearson's endorsed the traditional reading divisions between the sexes.

In discussing the ideology presented to women readers in these magazines, I will largely examine January 1923 issues, since the stories remain remarkably consistent throughout the run of the magazines. Despite some adjustments for readers of different classes, these magazines repeat the same romance narrative: a young heroine is "saved" from emotional or financial stress by a responsible young man who quickly becomes her husband.

The stress portrayed is emotional if the heroine is upper middle class and without need of money, as is Moyra Cassilis of "Toys and Love" (*The Royal*, Jan. 1923). A war widow turned flapper, Moyra is described as a "product of war restlessness, the froth flung to the surface by the world's chaos," i.e., a woman who possesses lapis lazuli cigarette cases and pearl rings yet suffers from spiritual emptiness.[31] At first unaware of her life's meaninglessness, she turns down a proposal from her intended savior, the solid Roger Boyd, an Australian farmer who longs to see "[her] wonder in the faces of [his] children"; however, she gratefully accepts his proposal after he saves her from the sexual advances of another suitor, the sinister Francis MacNaughten, an effete intellectual who fancies himself a poet.[32] Moyra's last words simultaneously affirm her need for the steady Roger Boyd and mark her rejection of the independent flapper life: "I do need you, now—and always."[33] Another such example is "Lynette the Plain One" (*Pearson's*, Jan. 1923), where the almost-thirty heroine, the youngest and plainest of five daughters, wins a suitor who finds her attractive and makes her feel young again by removing her worries over the family property (fig. 1.1).[34] Not only do these stories affirm the centrality of heterosexual romance, they also highlight women's traditional identification with submission and helplessness. These women may appear to be self-sufficient, yet by story's end their "true" need for dependency is revealed.

If the heroine is a working girl, more common in those magazines intended for working-class audiences such as *Peg's Paper*, she is saved from drudgery by her beloved. In "Was Her Husband False?" (*Peg's Paper*, 2 Jan. 1923), model Stephanie Verney is rescued from the unwelcome advances of Sir Clement by the intercession of handsome Trevor Lane, who marries her and sets her up in a "small house in one of the outer suburbs," where she enjoys the "glorious dream" of picking out new furnishings (fig. 1.2).[35] Having lost her modeling job through Sir Clement's meddling, Stephanie "succeeds" as wife, in her home called "The Haven."[36] Other narratives in the same issue are almost exact replicas of the lead story: a secretary making four pounds a week wins the love of her employer's nephew ("Her Sister's Sweetheart"), and a chorus girl finds a war veteran millionaire ("A Girl Should Never Tell").[37] The intended message of all these stories is hardly subtle: better to be a secure wife than an independent, but at-risk, working girl.

Both variants mark thinly disguised attacks on the "modern" girl, i.e., an independent-thinking woman with a job, as all these heroines possess

The lodger put his arm round Lynette. "To live in this beautiful house," he said dreamily, "to work a little, to play a little, and love—always."

Figure 1.1. From "Lynette the Plain One," *Pearson's Magazine*, January 1923, p. 57. By permission of The British Library. (PP 6004 gmq)

Figure 1.2. Cover of *Peg's Paper*, 2 January 1923. By permission of The British Library. (PP 6004 sal)

either an inward or an outward "old-fashionedness." In "Lynette the Plain One," the heroine is immediately recognizable as the prototypical old-fashioned girl, for her suitor remarks that her name reminds him "of singing birds and old-fashioned gardens."[38] But even the racy Moyra Cassilis from "Toys and Love," who possesses an avant-garde black bedroom with a red lacquer bed, is the daughter of "solid North Country Squires," whose memories of the country surface, despite repeated "jazzing" and champagne drinking.[39] These women's eventually vanquished rivals are unrepentant modern girls, like Jane from "Her Sister's Sweetheart," who briefly wins her sister's fiancé by producing a supposedly home-cooked meal that is really "ready-to-eat" food: "The things only required to be warmed up, and the extra expense was a mere detail to Jane."[40] Rejecting modernity (and its freedoms) is revealed to be woman's appropriate choice, as these heroines retain or recover their "true" natures and indeed nature itself, in Moyra's case by marrying an Australian farmer who takes her to the land of blue gum trees, or in Lynette's case by reclaiming the family garden, bought by her factory-owner husband.

These narratives hardly change in the decade that marks Smith's movement from young secretary to publishing writer. In "The Man Who Came Between" (*Peg's Paper,* 7 Jan. 1930), the penniless Rosalind Carfax, who sings on the streets to earn her living, is rescued by the opera promoter Maurice Laconda, only to be saved again from Laconda by the fiancé she thought dead, Gareth Lindsay. Nature again triumphs over culture, as Rosalind leaves London stage life for Gareth's estate in Scotland, metaphorically returning to her former life as a girl from a country cottage.[41] Jenny Lancaster, heroine of "Was It a Sin?" (*Peg's Paper,* 5 Jan. 1935), is saved by her employer, who forgives her small theft of company money, and finally marries her. Described as a "fresh, untouched . . . flower" (rather like the description of Lynette), Jenny is that same old-fashioned girl, whose loveliness "roused . . . all that was possessive and protective" in her suitor.[42] Despite the span of a decade, all the old gendered oppositions—dominance versus submission, nature versus culture—remain intact in these stories.

Perhaps the most frightening stories Smith would have encountered, however, were those that punished or deterred women from venturing out of their traditional roles. That Smith was familiar with these stories is made clear by her parody of one in *Novel on Yellow Paper.* Each of the women's magazines from January 1923 contained a story or feature intended to remind women of their places. For example, *Pearson's* "Her Night of Triumph" tells of a woman writer whose play is perceived as a flop until her ambitions are quelled and her priorities are reordered, symbolized by her return home and her nursing of her sick son. Having re-

gretted "offer[ing] up her loved ones on the altar of ambition," she is rewarded with a popular (not critical) success, her triumph consisting of her
newfound ability to take her son south for his health.[43] *The Royal* includes
a story called "Rosaleen Says Yes," in which an adventurous young woman
journalist sets out on a trip around the world, to get only as far as Hawaii,
where she falls in love and marries, thus ending her adventure rather
quickly.[44] *Peg's Companion* contains the feature story of an ambitious
young actress who thought she could live without marriage and family,
but found out she was wrong: "I began to feel that there was something
very comforting in the strength of a man's arm, especially when that arm
belonged to a special 'someone.'"[45] Perhaps the most amusing to a contemporary reader is a feature entitled "The Too-Independent Girl" in
Peg's Paper, in which Peg's male pal cautions a young woman against ap-
pearing too self-sufficient:

[Y]ou rely too much on yourself and don't allow Jack to help you in those little
things which are the delight of a man who is in love. One day last week I saw you
refuse his help when crossing a busy street. You see, Marion, you stifle the really
feminine part of your nature when you do that, and as the charm of every girl lies
in her femininity a man naturally feels awkward and stupid when she refuses his
help in little things.[46]

When she protests, saying, "I want to depend on myself," he scolds,
"Then Marion you ought not to be engaged. . . . You should not even have
a sweetheart."[47] Simultaneously lured and threatened, the women readers
of Pearson's magazines were given simple choices: lovely homes and brave
husbands versus pennilessness and the loss of femininity. These stories seldom support Billie Melman's conclusion in *Women and the Popular Imagination in the Twenties* that "the central, most salient feature of the twenties was the redefinition and remodelling of the woman's place."[48]
Though Melman concedes the conservatism of Pearson publications and
emphasizes the polyphonic nature of the decade's reading material, she
does not always credit the romance's conservative ideological force.

That Smith was aware of the ideology of domesticity and its potentially dangerous effect on women is made clear in her first published work,
Novel on Yellow Paper (1936). Yet such a reading is dependent on a fa-
miliarity with Smith's subversive narrative techniques. As she does frequently in her novels, Smith has her characters begin by agreeing with socially accepted opinions, only to gradually change their minds through a
process of reflection. To identify Smith with her characters, and not with
the process that her characters undergo, is to miss the work's "rhetorical
twists and turns," a phrase used by Shari Benstock to describe Virginia

Woolf's methodology in *Three Guineas*. Like Woolf, Smith mimes the rhetoric of patriarchy only to eventually subvert it.[49]

Smith's heroine, Pompey, begins her critique of women's magazines by excoriating the stupidity of women who are easily duped into the romantic desire for marriage and home; however, Pompey's scathing language soon blends into the language of the patriarchal capitalist who is dependent on these women for his livelihood:

> But it is their own fault. They ought to be drowned, they are so silly and make so much lamentation, and are wet, and are a burden. And are the public on whom we rely to buy and read our two-penny weeklies. And they do, they do. And that, Sir, is why we are able to pay a 15 per cent dividend on our ordinary shares and 10 per cent on the 2nd prefs. But you are too late too late at this time to try and get in on a good thing, because we are not selling, no we are holding on. And the only good thing these female half-wits ever did was to buy our publications and swell our dividends.[50]

Pompey's shift into her employer's language reveals that she has been taught to disassociate herself from the ideological mission of the business by placing responsibility on the customers, the female "half-wits" who buy the two-penny weeklies. Such a view champions an individualist, and capitalist, understanding of the world, where the individual is held completely responsible for her choices. But Pompey quickly falls out of this accusatory mode, as she comes to realize that the magazines themselves are in some way responsible for the attitudes of their women readers: "[T]hey are allowed to fill their little permanently waved heads with lovely lovely dreams of the never was. That I fear is where they get their funny thoughts on matrimony."[51]

Pompey completes her critique of the magazine industry's message of domesticity through a retelling of a typical magazine narrative.[52] Smith's "story" mimics the "warning" tale, a feature found in all the January 1923 magazines discussed above, although it does so in a highly subversive manner. In her retelling, a married woman is almost lured back into the public sphere of work by the visit of an unmarried friend, but changes her mind when her son, Tommy, knocks the stewpan over: "[S]o the wife thinks: I very nearly left my lovely Home, my lovely Tommy, my lovely husband."[53] Pompey's telling of the story reveals frequent gaps or silences, when her sentence trails off, sometimes ending in an ellipsis, at others ending in an abrupt period. Such gaps indicate the junctures in the story where Pompey begins to question what she has formerly believed. Pompey, who had earlier been so critical of the women magazine readers, concludes her analysis by saying: "You can pay too much for a good dividend."[54] Here

14

she replaces her previous conclusion, that the "female half-wits" are needed to maintain dividends, with one that is finally critical of the magazine business in its manipulation of women for profit.

Smith asserts that women's desire for marriage draws them into a web of consumption, first as unmarried women trying to win husbands with "a spot of scent behind the ear," then as married women focused on domestic objects, which Smith refers to as the "little bright twopenny clockword toy[s]" that women "[see] through [their] wedding ring[s]."[55] For Smith, the goal of marriage, really the goal of the perfectly furnished home, is finally unsatisfying and merely masks the real labor involved in married life:

Sure enough Miss Snooks has got married to that nice solid young fellow. But somehow the gilt is off the gingerbread. It is all washing up and peeling potatoes, and there are several *kiddies,* and the furniture isn't paid for, and is already beginning to look like it was time for some more. And oh how dim drab and dreary is life in terms of squawling brats and cash instalments.[56]

Smith's condemnation of consumer culture may seem dated in light of recent analyses of women and consumerism that emphasize the joy and power women can receive from spending.[57] Yet, Smith's analysis needs to be centered in the culture of the thirties, when women's newly earned ability to receive wages of their own was steadily being eroded, when new timesaving devices failed to save time, and when remaining single was increasingly vilified.[58]

The intersection of women and consumerism is hardly a simple one for Smith, as is revealed in her lengthy description of Harriet's flat in *Novel on Yellow Paper.* Despite its "artsy" appearance, a reflection of Harriet's taste and her earning potential as a single professional, heroine Pompey sees in its coziness a desire for domesticity that matches that of Harriet's magazine readers:

Harriet has a flat in Clarence Mansions on the second floor. The furniture is silvered oak and the colour scheme—this reminds me of readers' letters. They write in 'from the north of England': I have taken a house, it is called "Fairlight," it is semi-detached, can you give me a colour scheme for sitting room, kitchen, best bedroom and drawing room.[59]

In Pompey's ambivalence over Harriet's flat—her simultaneous admiration and boredom—we can see Smith's own ambivalence, as Pompey's experiences with Harriet are based on those of Smith with Narcissa Crowe-Wood. Smith admires the talent of those such as Harriet who use their surroundings to express personality; yet she fears that Harriet's admittedly lovely product is nonetheless tied to cultural mandates on femininity and domesticity. Additionally, Smith acknowledges the comfort that homemaking provides for guests, in this case, Pompey; yet such a skill obviously makes Pompey (and Smith) feel inadequate, on both gender and class grounds.

Smith's ambivalent attitudes remind us what "buying" meant for a woman of a particular class, in a particular period. Analyses of consuming must acknowledge their sometimes limited historicity; shopping may have provided nineteenth-century women with the ability to escape the domestic sphere, and contemporary green consumerism may pose a method of freedom, but these are particularized instances.[60] Buying in the thirties presented complex, and not nearly so positive, meanings for Smith. As Rita Felski suggests in *The Gender of Modernity,* "the celebration of the resistive agency of the female consumer is currently in danger of becoming a new orthodoxy."[61] Though representing only one point of view from her period, Smith was to see consumerism and domesticity as inextricably connected in hindering women's freedoms.

A RESISTANT METHODOLOGY

In *Novel on Yellow Paper,* Smith appears to assume that the ideology of women's magazines directly controls its women readers by luring them into domestic lifestyles. Her concern over women's vulnerability to reading material would seem to draw her closer to Victorian social and medical commentators, fearful of women's extreme sensitivity and susceptibility, than to recent critics of popular culture.[62] For example, Janice Radway and Angela McRobbie maintain that women readers/viewers have the ability to resist and transform cultural representation. In her study of romance readers, Radway found that the reading of romances was both "combative and compensatory" because time spent reading marks a rejection of women's self-abnegating role and because romances, which validate love and personal interaction, are strongly opposed to the masculine values of competition and public achievement. She concludes her study with a cautious, but positive, interpretation of romance reading: "[A]lthough the ideological power of contemporary cultural forms is enormous, indeed sometimes even frightening, that power is not yet all-pervasive, totally vigilant, or complete."[63] McRobbie, who is more wary than Radway of the "feminine plots" common to popular British teen magazines *Jackie* and *My Guy,* nevertheless finds alternative forms of popular culture, such as the films *Flashdance* and *Fame,* offering value systems other than the domestic.[64] Smith's apparent elitist, modernist dread of all that is popular, as expressed in *Novel on Yellow Paper,* would seem to op-

Introduction

pose Radway's and McRobbie's sense of a multifaceted culture. Yet Smith's own radical retellings in *Novel,* as well as statements in later works, suggest that she saw texts and/or visual art, to use Thomas Leitch's terminology, as "projecting" or "predicting" responses rather than "inscribing" them.[65] Her critique led her, as have Leitch's, "to explore the continuities between [her] response and that of the audience."[66]

Like Radway, Smith did not believe that culture has complete control over a reading public. Smith herself was an eclectic, opinionated reader and continually defended readers against encroachment from institutional judges, such as editors and literary critics. In Smith's last novel, *The Holiday,* her character Celia suggests that writers do not have total power over their audiences, for their ideas must be sorted out "by the sifting process of the judging mind of the reader."[67] That Celia, in this instance, shares the opinions of Smith is revealed in Smith's most famous essay, "History or Poetic Drama?" (1958). In the essay, Smith rejects Eliot's hierarchical worldview in *Murder in the Cathedral,* yet asserts that "he stirs our thoughts and does no harm, if our minds are cool he does not harm but gives pleasure."[68] For Smith, the "cool" mind was a resisting one. These comments suggest that she hardly saw readers as passive sponges.

And like McRobbie, Smith believed that culture was anything but monolithic. In her book columns written from 1941 to 1951 in the largely conservative magazine *Modern Woman,* Smith attempted to disrupt the influence of domestic ideology on her women readers by recommending not only romances but a wide variety of reading. She apparently felt that the romance plot's influence would decline if women encountered other genres. Here Smith would seem to be following in the footsteps of Victorian forbears, some of them feminists, who attempted to draw women away from the romance by introducing them to other possibilities.[69] A reader of a great variety of literature, Smith countered the apparent monolith of domestic ideology with other forms of culture.

Smith's remarks on the relative susceptibility of readers to the influence of mass culture appear contradictory, yet are not so if read in the light of an ideological theory that takes into account culture as a complex field of competing discourses, some of which possess greater dominance than others. Although Smith never expressed anything approaching a full-blown theory of ideology, her above remarks on readers and reading suggest a certain affinity with Bakhtinian concepts of culture. Bakhtin's notion that culture is characterized by "a multitude of bounded verbal-ideological and social belief systems," or heteroglossia, would have come as no surprise to a woman writer who was a constant traveler through an almost bewildering array of past and then-present discourse groups.[70] As might be expected, she drew from her romantic and Victorian forefa-

17

thers: Blake, Tennyson, and Browning. Yet she also responded to the experimental work of Dorothy Richardson and Virginia Woolf, the satire of Dorothy Parker and Anita Loos, the drawings of Edward Lear, the music hall tradition, Anglican church hymns, folktales, fairy stories, and advertisements in popular magazines. Throughout her life, she moved through, and enjoyed, a diversity of social circles: the middle-class life of Palmer's Green, the left intellectual circle of Margaret Gardiner and others, the marginalized women novelists whom she called "academic girls," the country house circle of the landed gentry, and, tangentially, the aristocratic life of her employers. Smith, who made use of American slang as well as a multitude of different British dialects, was a collector of diverse discourses.

Not that she valued all discourses equally, as is revealed by her extreme suspicion of domestic ideology in *Novel on Yellow Paper*, and in later works. Like Bakhtin, she seems to have believed that culture was composed of centripetal and centrifugal forces: "Alongside the centripetal forces, the centrifugal forces of language carry on their uninterrupted work; alongside verbal-ideological centralization and unification, the uninterrupted processes of decentralization and disunification go forward."[71] Drawing on centrifugal forces as diverse as the music hall and Edward Lear's drawings, Smith's work was to act as one of the mechanisms of "decentralization and disunification" in a culture that was increasingly unifying around the concept of domestic ideology. She was to combat the forces of centralization through two of the three mechanisms elaborated in Bakhtin's work on Rabelais: parody and carnival.[72]

Like Luce Irigaray and other feminist critics, Smith uses retelling, or mimicry, to parody dominant discourses. According to Irigaray, the woman who would challenge "reasonable" words must "carry back, reimport, those crises that her 'body' suffers in her impotence to say what disturbs her."[73] Smith's fictional retellings of popular magazine stories and classics such as *The Bacchae*, as well as critical retellings of romance novels, are similar to Irigaray's rerenderings of Freud, Plato, and Plotinus in her early work, *Speculum*. In addition, Smith was to reinscribe images of womanhood in her performances by dressing up as young ingenues. Although Toril Moi is skeptical of the success of mimicry, she describes its intended effect:

. . . Irigaray's mimicry in *Speculum* becomes a conscious acting out of the hysteric (mimetic) position allocated to all women under patriarchy. Through her acceptance of what is in any case an ineluctable mimicry, Irigaray doubles it back on itself, thus raising the parasitism to the second power. Hers is a theatrical staging of the mime: miming the miming imposed on woman. Irigaray's subtle specular move (her mimicry mirrors that of all women) intends to *undo* the effects of phallo-centric discourse simply by *overdoing* them. . . .[74]

Moi's fear is that this parodic strategy will lead to replaying rather than disrupting culture. But Gail Schwab, who has linked Irigaray to the Bakhtinian tradition of dialogism, points out that this is only *one* element in Irigaray's bag of rhetorical tricks, just as it is only one means by which Smith opposed her culture.[75] Both Smith and Irigaray are writers who make use of a wide variety of rhetorical strategies, from the subversive to the direct.

The carnivalesque nature of Smith's work requires challenging for-malist as well as biographical readings. Though the former are not as prevalent, some have tried to limit Smith's work to the printed word. Once Smith is recovered from the formalist tradition that excised her sung poems and her drawings, as well as downplayed the range of her influ-ences and sources, we can see that her work, which exuberantly mixes "high" and "low" art forms, epitomizes what Bakhtin has called the car-nivalesque, the mixture of serious and comic levels of art. Smith's art re-quires an audience to make sense of its many incongruities: the amateur-ish, often comic drawings mixed with her poems, the off-key tunes to which she sings her poems, the jumble of experimental and popular forms in her fiction, and the wide range of books included in her reviews. The response to her work is often laughter, which according to Bakhtin has the potential to disrupt hierarchical order. Her work directly challenges both the literary and the social order, a fact that no doubt contributed to Smith's lack of a publisher in the fifties.

In her use of a multitude of discourses and media, Smith resembles another master of the carnivalesque, her contemporary Bertolt Brecht. As did Smith, Brecht based his art work on startling juxtapositions:

. . . Brecht . . . encouraged the use of montage, disruption of narrative, refusal of identifications with heroes and heroines, the intermingling of modes from high and popular culture, the use of different registers such as the comic, tragic as well as a confection of songs, images, sounds, film, and so forth. Complex seeing and complex multilayered texts were the project.[76]

Following Stephen Heath, Griselda Pollock translates this technique as distanciation rather than the more-familiar alienation, since the artist's goal is to heighten viewers' attention and thereby "distance" them from social order, not remove them from involvement. Stephen Heath traces distanciation to Brecht's admiration of Chinese art, which places images side by side, and thus avoids the hierarchical nature of Western art by re-

19

quiring the reader/viewer to make sense of the split-screen effect.[77] Because of her art's juxtaposition of forms, Smith needs to be recovered, as has Brecht himself, as one of a diverse community of writers and artists who have contributed directly, or indirectly, to postmodernism.[78] Indeed, an examination of postmodernism can illuminate the work of Smith.

One of the unfortunate tendencies of recent work on Smith is the sole concentration on her poetry, which involves ignoring some of her more daring attempts at what Linda Hutcheon has called "border-line inquiries," or the crossing of traditionally distinct genres and medias. Hutcheon sees the transgression of traditional literary and artistic boundaries as one of the fundamental traits of postmodernism:

It upsets learned notions of the relations between text/image, non-art/art, theory/practice—by installing the conventions of both (which are often taken for granted) and then by investigating the borders along which each can be opened, subverted, altered by the other in new ways. This typically postmodern border tension between inscription and subversion, construction and deconstruction— within the art itself—also places demands upon critics and their means of approaching such works. And, one of the most insistent of these demands involves a coming to terms with the theoretical and political implications of what has too often been seen as an empty, formal play of codes.[79]

The code-breaking or play aspect, of Smith's work has been acknowledged, yet its multiple transgressions, and their consequences, have not.[80] Known mainly as a poet, Smith needs to be recovered as an artist who worked in visual art and music, as well as a variety of literary forms.

Such a mixture of normally distinct elements creates an open-ended art form, one that must necessarily create a new, and active, relationship between the artist and his or her audience. According to Linda Hutcheon,

[P]ostmodernism . . . values process ("the course") over product ("the finish"), the text qua formal text has no fixed and final value in and for itself. It is not a closed and fetishized object, but an open process with an enunciative situation that changes with each receiver. . . .[81]

Receivers are thus crucial to postmodern art, since artists rely on them to decode their challenges to convention. As is illustrated in her statements on readers and reading, Smith had faith in the ability of her readers/ viewers to challenge conventions, and her difficult though playful art often requires them to do so.

Although Hutcheon cautions that postmodernism's tendency to "install" as well as "subvert" leaves it open to reactionary as well as progressive tendencies, she suggests that this new relationship between artist and reader, one that requires the reader to question socially accepted boundaries, is what gives postmodernism the possibility to promote change:

> Postmodern culture, then, has a contradictory relationship to what we usually label our dominant, liberal humanist culture. It does not deny it, as some have asserted. . . . Instead, it contests it from within its own assumptions. . . .
> . . . What is important in all these internalized challenges to humanism is the interrogating of the notion of consensus. . . . In its most extreme formulation, the result is that consensus becomes the illusion of consensus. . . .[82]

It is this illusion of consensus, or the unity of beliefs, that Smith's caustic art was so often to challenge.

BOUNDARY-CROSSING ART FORMS

Smith's art works against many forms of consensus—what is adult, what is moral, what is literary, what is religious—and many of these challenges have been examined in previous studies. But perhaps her most radical challenge is of definitions of femininity. Through her "re"-performance of the romance, actually a "mis"-performance in its mixing of incongruous forms of representation, Smith was to challenge the unity and coherence of women's gender identity. As Judith Butler has suggested, it is through "reiteration that gaps and fissures are opened up as . . . constitutive instabilities."[83]

In her novels, begun during the thirties, Smith borrows the experimental, antilinear techniques of foremothers Dorothy Richardson and Virginia Woolf to disrupt the return of Victorian separate-spheres ideology in a Britain affected by the Slump. Crossing women's "high" art with mass culture, Smith uses experimental prose intrusions, as well as Richardson's and Woolf's communal plotting, against the romance. Yet Smith finally preserves the romance in order to critique its prominence and sway.

Also beginning in the thirties, Smith undermines lyric renderings of the romance with her comic drawings, as well as using caustic lyrics against idealized visual depictions of domestic ideology as presented in contemporary women's magazines. Relying on a tradition drawn from William Blake and Edward Lear, Smith uses the conventions of the two art forms against each other.

In her book reviews written for *Modern Woman* during World War II, Smith was to disrupt the domestic normalcy of the magazine's offerings, something of an oddity in the forties, with reviews of works that encouraged women readers to see themselves and the war differently. Her satiric reviews of romances serve to parody and mock romance conventions. In addition, Smith challenges the magazine's romance content with a wide variety of popular genres, such as the mystery and the children's book, but also middlebrow women's fiction written by friends such as Inez Holden and Olivia Manning, as well as some works in the "high" art tradition.

In her short stories, written largely during the 1950s wave of conservative gender ideology, Smith was to rely on the liberating tradition of 1920s women satirists such as Anita Loos and Dorothy Parker. Unlike male satirists Aldous Huxley and Evelyn Waugh, whose satire is nostalgic in its longing for traditional gender roles, Loos, Parker, and Smith use satire to poke fun at a world constructed around gender divisions. But Smith's art goes farther than that of Loos and Parker in that its satire is finally fantastic rather than tragic. Smith's satire manages to vault out of the present into a fantastic mode, which serves as a way of envisioning new roles.

In her sung poems, performed largely during the sixties, Smith used the Victorian music hall tradition to further movements away from conservative definitions of femininity. Frequently, her sung poems challenge social texts through musical parody. Also, mournful songs add sympathy to caustic poems, thereby enabling Smith to critique ideology yet exhibit sympathy for those women who have conformed to it. In this other example of media crossing, Smith pits the destabilizing tradition of performance against that of literature's supposed timeless permanence.

All of these boundary crossings reveal a writer who pulled from a vast array of sources. Although Smith made use of the parodic and carnivalesque *techniques* of what Bakhtin has called folk culture, she did not rely solely on the centrifugal force of folk culture itself. Smith did use folk songs and folk stories against domestic ideology, but she used a wide variety of cultural forms as well. Through this diversity, Smith avoided the nostalgia for the past, or at the very least, overidealization of folk culture, that Bakhtin has sometimes been criticized for.[84] Smith did not use past cultural forms against the present in an effort to regain the past, imaginary or otherwise. Rather, she used any centrifugal force available, past or present, "high" or "low." In her playful and varied use of sources, Smith can be considered a more apt practitioner of Bakhtinian dialogics than Bakhtin himself.

Although Smith's biographers have suggested that her politics were largely conservative, her composite art form reveals her commentary on gender to be radical in comparison with that of many interwar women writers, who were increasingly comfortable with images of domesticity. For example, Alison Light, in *Forever England,* has suggested that Ivy

Compton-Burnett, Agatha Christie, Jan Struthers (through her Mrs. Miniver columns), and Daphne du Maurier managed to critique Victorian gender roles while at the same time embracing domestic ideology.[85] Smith, however, could not find such divergent views compatible. Although Smith herself often enjoyed being cosseted and cared for at the homes of married friends, she was just as glad to leave them again. And her work is consistently critical of interwar and post-World War II definitions of romance and marriage, which she saw as leading to women's subordination. Studying Smith's boundary-crossing art forms involves recovering another voice in, and another woman's opinions on, this period's dialogue concerning domesticity. To portray Smith's dissension is not to cast her as feminist heroine, a role that, as Light remarks, fails to take into account the ways in which culture binds, but to recover her radicalism vis-à-vis her cultural context.[86] In so doing, this study continues the illumination of a still-dark period of literary history, British women's writing from 1930 to 1960. But Smith's art also must be seen as pointing to the future, since her techniques for disrupting domestic ideology are those currently at work in the feminist postmodernism of the visual and performance arts. As an artist who chose Hermes, the traveler, to signify her muse, Smith leads us backward and forward through discussions on women and cultural representation.[87]

2

The Novels
1936–1949

Until the last two decades of her life, Stevie Smith was as widely known for her novels as for her now more famous poems and drawings. *Novel on Yellow Paper* (1936) launched her career and continued to earn her enthusiastic fans for the rest of her life. Her other two novels, *Over the Frontier* (1938) and *The Holiday* (1949), also received critical acclaim, especially the latter, Smith's personal favorite.[1] Given the popularity of these works, a contemporary reader might easily expect to find them lighthearted and comic. And indeed, the novels are wickedly funny, but they are also dense and difficult, bewildering in their plot disruptions and dislocations. Kathleen Wheeler, the first critic to concentrate solely on Smith's novels, attests that they are marked by "an intense and disruptive impatience with established forms."[2] However, Smith's experiments in the novel form have been largely neglected, even in feminist recovery work. For example, Elaine Showalter claims that women novelists of the 1930s "rejected much of the experimentation of modernism" and fails to mention Smith in either the text or the biographical appendix of *A Literature of Their Own* (1977).[3] A more recent example, Ellen Friedman and Miriam Fuchs's *Breaking the Sequence* (1989), addresses "the neglect of women innovators" in literary histories of twentieth-century experimental fiction by providing an alternative tradition, yet Smith's work is not featured, nor does she figure in the book's extensive bibliography.[4]

Despite this omission, Friedman and Fuchs's work is invaluable to a study of Smith in that it provides a historical tradition of women's experimental writing, without which Smith's puzzling and difficult novels might easily seem incoherent. According to their historical mapping, Smith falls into the second generation of experimental women writers (1930–60), a placement that uncovers her debt to key figures in the first: Dorothy Richardson and Virginia Woolf. Although Smith's early reviewers linked her work to that of a number of writers, including Gertrude Stein, the eighteenth-century novelist Laurence Sterne, and American satirist Anita Loos, Smith's journals and library reveal her to have been as much, if not more, influenced by her female compatriots.[5] Smith's journals from the twenties document that she had read Richardson and many of Woolf's works—*The Common Reader, Mrs. Dalloway,* and *Orlando*—long before she began her career as a novelist.[6] Smith may have borrowed her Americanisms from Dorothy Parker, but it is her antilinear disruption of traditional romantic narratives that links her to the subversive stylistics of Richardson and Woolf. Indeed, Wheeler finds that her "commitment to experimentation makes her one with the [women] pre-modernists and modernists immediately preceding her."[7] When centered in this tradition, Smith's novels no longer appear difficult or eccentric, though her boundary crossing, more postmodern than modern, is unique except perhaps for Woolf's later works.

Like Richardson's and Woolf's works, Smith's novels mark a revolt against Victorianism, with its restrictive definitions of femininity.[8] In *Novel on Yellow Paper,* Smith's alter ego Pompey associates Victorian novels with her "paternal grandfather's library at Scaithness," thereby tying the novels' ideology to the family patriarch, though patriarchs in Pompey's family (as in Smith's) are few and far between.[9] Pompey fears that she has "read too much," i.e., that she is profoundly under the sway of the novels' dated messages.[10] But Pompey's narrative reveals her author, at least, to be more resistant to the popular Victorian novel.

Smith cites two popular novels that exemplify her understanding of Victoriana, one *Mrs. Halliburton's Troubles,* by the famous Victorian novelist Mrs. Humphry Ward, and the other *Lost Sir Massingberd,* by James Payn.[11] The predecessors of the romantic and adventure novels of Smith's day, just as Victorian women's magazines evolved into publications such as *Peg's Paper,* these Victorian novels serve up narratives based on a rigid distinction of gender roles. Although Pompey playfully professes admiration for both books, claiming a love for "damp Victorian troubles," Smith's entire narrative is pitted against the conventions they represent.[12] Pompey remembers the novels only after considering the pacing of her own book, which she compares to her horse's "hatred and panic at the white gate posts."[13] Indeed, it is this hatred and panic at "gate posts," or narrative conventions, that she claims "is the thought of all I wish to say in this book."[14] Part of this hatred has to do with the explicit gendering of the named narratives, as is evidenced by the fact that she

25

mocks the linear patterning of both a woman's novel and a man's adventure-mystery.

Though not a romance, *Mrs. Halliburton's Troubles* is a typically domestic-driven novel in that it portrays Mrs. Jane Halliburton's slow recovery of her home and security, threatened after her husband's premature death. Because of her poverty, she must work, but she sews gloves at home, thus never leaving her family unattended and retaining her middle-class status. Her trials and troubles shake, but never completely disrupt, her fidelity to domestic ideology. As one who recognizes her subordinate position, she relies solely on the judgment and guidance of other patriarchs: God, her sympathetic landlord, and finally, her sons. The novel ends with Mrs. Halliburton, her three sons having achieved respectability and wealth, about to live out her days with one of them, a vicar, who replaces her clerical father and clerically intended schoolmaster husband. By remaining faithful to her domestic role, Mrs. Halliburton is given back the domestic reward of security, of being "kept." As Smith points out, the novel is linear, motivated by Mrs. Halliburton's faith in God; Mrs. Halliburton's God just happens to mete out rewards based on predictably gendered plots.[15]

Providence, Smith's word for a novel's linear drive to an ending, is equally manifest in the second novel Smith names, *Lost Sir Massingberd,* but here Providence provides a predictably different ending, since this is a mystery-adventure story, with males as its main characters. Despite the hero Marmaduke Heath's fear of continuing his uncle's evil dynasty, he eventually marries and moves into the family estate, continuing the family line and the rule of the patriarch. While Mrs. Halliburton is rewarded with safety and security, Marmaduke Heath is given the power of position and the care of a wife. Both novels are, as Pompey suggests, "tidy," and thus predictable in their movements, especially in the gendering of their narrative lines.[16]

Yet these novels are finally somewhat unusual choices of Victoriana and might have been read, by Smith and others, more subversively. Smith does not say why she chose to feature these particular novels, out of the many examples she might have picked, but perhaps she names them because they both expose the extreme vulnerability of married women under a patriarchal system, fear of which prevents her heroine Pompey from ever marrying. The poverty resulting from the death of Mrs. Halliburton's husband reveals women's and children's insecurity under the supposedly secure patriarchal system. Jane Halliburton survives, but her "double," daughter Jane, perishes from malnutrition and illness. *Lost Sir Massingberd,* a curious rewrite of *Jane Eyre,* is also somewhat murky in its message: Old Sir Massingberd's violence against his young gypsy wife, who is driven mad and then locked up, leads us to question not only him but the entire system he represents. Although the young and seemingly good Marmaduke Heath, the new Sir Massingberd, survives to take his blonde young bride to the estate, the novel is nevertheless unsettling—after all, Marmaduke himself claims that "our family residence is consecrated to the devil."[17]

Despite their ambivalent ideologies, the texts behind Smith's *Novel on Yellow Paper* reveal a historical tradition of gendered narratives, a tradition that Smith criticizes through her writing of three novels that defy their conventions. In the opening of *Novel on Yellow Paper,* Smith claims that she is writing a "not-book," meaning a book that is not a magazine, or not a romantic woman's plot, but her novel is also a "not-book" in that it is unrecognizable by Victorian standards.[18]

But why should Smith have felt this need to vilify Victorian convention in the late 1930s? Hadn't the first generation of women experimentalists already swept aside stultifying conventions, leaving her a clear and empty space? What we find from Smith's narratives and other historical accounts is that Victorianism was by no means swept away in the 1930s. In fact, the late 1930s mark a revival of the separate-spheres concept and a return to traditional notions of femininity. Virginia Woolf documents this intensifying backlash in *Three Guineas,* when she cites several *Daily Telegraph* quotations from 1936, the year Smith published her novel. One of Woolf's male voices is particularly noteworthy because of his assurance that his beliefs are widespread:

I am certain I voice the opinion of thousands of young men when I say that if men were doing the work that thousands of young women are now doing the men would be able to keep those same women in decent homes. Homes are the real places of the women who are now compelling men to be idle. It is time the Government insisted upon employers giving work to more men, thus enabling them to marry the women they cannot now approach.[19]

In his certainty that women belong in the home and that men must necessarily function as breadwinners, this young man is not so far away from his Victorian father and grandfather. Frightened by the economics of the Slump and perhaps the threat of women's future gains in upcoming wars, this man relies, somewhat wistfully, on the settled views of the past. Red velvet draperies might be out of style in 1936, but the psychology of Victorianism was again fashionable.

Repeating the work of her foremothers, Smith sought to move beyond the limitations of Victorian and popular narratives by assaulting their gender-driven pacing, particularly the domestic-oriented linearity of the

woman's novel. *Novel on Yellow Paper* starts Pompey out on a love journey, but it is hardly a predictable one, since it strays frequently from romance and continues past the boundaries of an individual novel. Smith
may have borrowed this notion of the continuing saga from Dorothy
Richardson's many-volumed *Pilgrimage*. Although not nearly as long-
winded as Richardson, Smith did produce a series of three novels that can
be read as one continuing story. The first two novels retain the same narrator, Pompey, and as many have pointed out, Celia, *The Holiday*'s story-
teller, is almost indistinguishable from Pompey. For example, Joyce Carol
Oates, in a 1982 review of the three reprinted novels, claims that Celia is
"clearly a close relation" of Pompey.[20] Of course, Smith could, conceiv-
ably, have inherited this technique from that equally long-winded French-
man Marcel Proust, who had also been on Smith's reading list. But Smith's
use of the continuing saga fulfills the same function as it does in Richardson's novels: It prevents closure. Smith's novels, like both Richardson's
and Woolf's, form one long assault on the romance plot in that they
refuse the closure of that most suitable of endings, marriage.

Yet Smith's novels are still recognizable as belonging to one of her generation and, specifically, a woman of lower-middle-class origins. As
Rachel DuPlessis attests in *Writing beyond the Ending*, Richardson and
Woolf largely jettisoned the romance plot, using their fiction to explore
communal rather than familial structures.[21] Far from leaving the romance
behind, Smith's first two novels combine a recognizable romance plot with
experimentation. One has to wonder why Smith felt it necessary to return,
at least partially, to the romance. The answer would seem to lie in Smith's
class positioning. As Alison Light suggests, the interwar years were characterized by a downmarketing of the romance:

The meanings of romance and of 'romantic' as terms of literary description became more narrowly specialized between the wars, coming to signify only those
love-stories, aimed ostensibly at a wholly female readership, which deal primarily
with the trials and tribulations of heterosexual desire, and end happily in marriage.
At the same time, there is a sense in which, as part of the creation of this 'genre,'
romance went downmarket as it was boosted by the growth in forms of 'mass entertainment' in the period and its commercialisation made it a bestselling form for
a much larger group of readers.[22]

A secretary who had not attended university, Smith may have felt the need
to disassociate herself from the genre's class implications through a direct
attack, as well as to acknowledge the form's power over its women readers.
Although Smith's Pompey trashes romantic reading, she finds herself sus-
ceptible to its draw. When she gives in to romantic delusions with Karl and

Freddy, she envisions herself actually inside a Mrs. Humphry Ward novel, groping with Karl in a Ward-ish house, kissing with Freddy in a Ward-ish gaslight scene. By conjoining the romance with the experimental women's novel, Smith throws the two genres into dialogue with each other.

This crossing of genres, the popular romance with the experimental women's novel, forces readers to consider the boundaries and the implications of each form. Through her use of the romance, Smith reveals that restrictive ideologies still exist for women, despite the disruptive attempts of the first generation of women modernists. Smith's "pollution" of "high" art forms suggests that experimental women's novels must take on the entire question of literary hierarchy, including why so few women were able to enter the "high" art world and what entering that world means in terms of one's audience. Thus, Smith was directly to confront the challenge common to many women writers concerned with depictions of femininity, that which Mary Poovey describes as the simultaneous recognition of woman as a theoretical concept and women as specific, historic beings:

The challenge for those of us who are convinced both that real historical women do exist and share certain experiences and that deconstruction's demystification of presence makes theoretical sense is to work out some way to think both women and "woman."[23]

Smith may have read *Mrs. Dalloway* and *Orlando,* but the works in which she most resembles Woolf are *Three Guineas* and *The Years* (originally intended to combine news and fiction), works that directly address a writer's responsibility to work across media and readership boundaries.

Smith's first two novels are romance stories literally cut with experimental sections or interruptions. These two early works share nothing of the smooth organicism of Richardson's and Woolf's "feminine" writing styles. At first fairly brief and insignificant, the interruptions in Smith's novels grow progressively longer and more disruptive.

Novel on Yellow Paper contains many small blips in the narrative: inserted quotations, fantasies, and retellings of classics. Smith herself gives us a way of envisioning the course of her narrative through the horses in the trilogy, which become metaphors for pacing. *Novel on Yellow Paper* begins with her riding on a sedate horse who dances "between the posts," i.e., reluctantly follows the rules, but she remembers once riding another horse, Kismet, who refused to follow any course. Smith sees herself as a composite of the sedate, convention-bound horse, the wild Kismet who transgresses rules, and these horses' rider, the one who can "pull up," that is, control both the flow of the conventional narrative and the radical digressions.[24]

Smith's intercuts after *Novel on Yellow Paper* grow increasingly lengthy, however, as the heroine struggles more effectively against the romance plot, despite higher odds. In *Over the Frontier,* Pompey almost succumbs to the dysphoric ending of the romance plot, as her love for Freddy begins to weaken her, almost to the point of death, but her clever creator rescues her through splicing the man's adventure story onto the end of *Over the Frontier.* This ending baffled contemporary critics, but its point becomes clearer if we realize that Smith was using the masculine adventure story as a weapon against the romance plot. The horse metaphor for this novel is appropriated from a George Grosz painting, entitled *Haute Ecole,* its horse and rider drawing Pompey to consider masculinity and its connection to the last war's violence. Seizing masculinity for her own, Pompey emerges in a military uniform and thus escapes the fate of marrying the hale and hearty Tom Satterthwaite. Her retreat into masculinity is temporary, however, as she discovers the price to be paid for lingering too long near the masculine gate post.

The novel where Smith most resembles her foremothers is *The Holiday* (1949), published significantly later than her first two. In *The Holiday,* she departs from her romantic/experimental cross and explores the alternative communal plotting common to Richardson and Woolf. Here the Pompey double, Celia, challenges both the romance and the quest plot by opting out of oedipal patterns. However, the entire novel can be read as an intercut into Pompey's story, as Smith renames Pompey Celia and sends her on "holiday." Boundary crossing, Smith would seem to suggest, must eventually result in the dissolution of boundaries and in alternatives to a boundary-driven world. Like Woolf in *The Years* (1937), Smith links her nonlinear and nongendered narrative to an ideological purpose: restructuring our most basic social patterns. Although both women writers believe that new social patterns are essential for our collective survival, Smith is finally less optimistic than Woolf about derailing a rigidly gendered society, since psychic patterns replay themselves.

ASSAULT ON THE ROMANCE TRADITION IN
NOVEL ON YELLOW PAPER

Despite the narrative's twists and turns, *Novel on Yellow Paper* must be read as something of a romance: Smith's heroine Pompey falls in love with a German student named Karl, then a fellow London suburbanite, Freddy. With its two loves, one more passionate, the other more serious and steady, the novel would seem to be a rewriting of a story from a Pearson's publication, where the heroine eventually chooses the more steady male.[25] We expect Pompey to end up with the stolid Freddy and settle into her role as comfortable suburbanite matron.

30

But this simple, linear story is hardly the narrative the reader receives. In fact, Smith warns her readers that if they are looking for the typical rags-to-riches romance they can "shut up here and throw back at Miss-in-Boots cash chemists book-store."[26] Supposedly typed by Smith on yellow paper supplied by her employer, *Novel* is anything but predictable. The emphasis on yellow in the title links Smith's book back to those of the groundbreaking New Woman novelists, since their books, issued in single form rather than as the more popular three-decker, were associated with the scurrilous and scandalous yellow-backs of the 1860s.[27] Linked to an even earlier experimentalism than that of Richardson and Woolf, *Novel* follows in a long line of women's novels resistant to traditional notions of femininity.[28] Yellow is also frequently associated with madness, and *Novel,* with its many digressions, is something of a mad book. One of the main literary allusions of *Novel* is, after all, that of *The Bacchae,* where Dionysus incites the Theban women to run wild.

Smith's main weapon against the romance is the digressive intercut. Through these intercuts, Smith (and Pompey) reveal that they are not to be coded through the traditional romance, but are expert coders in their own right. As Wheeler points out, coding becomes a metaphor for reading and interpretation, a talent Pompey has inherited from her father, whose mysterious profession has something to do with his language ability:

My papa was, among many other duties, in charge of the coding department. And very highly complicated it was, and I often think of him with very real sympathy when I am doing our own, by no means simple, coding at the office.[29]

Here Pompey—and through Pompey, Smith—claims language for her own, rejecting any association with traditional feminine inarticulation, as well as feminine coded pathways of romance. As Kristeva suggests, and Smith understands, the symbolic cannot be rejected if a woman writer is to make an impact: "[M]asculine, paternal identification, because it supports symbol and time, is necessary in order to have a voice in the chapter of politics and history."[30]

One of the potentially most baffling types of intercuts in *Novel* is the quotations, occasionally chapters of them, that literally stall the narrative. These passages, which read like a writer's journal, are often indeed from Smith's journals, the notebooks she kept for ten years before she began publishing. Unable and unwilling to obtain a university education, Smith was to educate herself through extensive reading and the writing of these notebooks. Here Smith appears to have been influenced by the educational practices advocated by Victorian commentators, who suggested that women readers might improve their abilities by copying passages.[31]

Her notebooks therefore become a sign of Smith's control over language, her theft of an education, since she was able to become a writer without the normal institutional training. As Jane Marcus points out in "Thinking Back through Our Mothers," the introduction to *New Feminist Essays on Virginia Woolf,* both Walter Benjamin and Virginia Woolf similarly kept notebooks in order to rob culture of its history.[32] In Smith's case, the quotations act as a demonstration of her learning and her ability to use it against the culture that assigned her to the role of romance, since the quotations literally stop or block Pompey from her romance journey toward marriage.

Journal keeping uncovers at least one method for resisting the culture; through the process of copying over passages, the woman writer turns the culture into a word salad. When narrative's protective covering is carved away, isolated phrases stand out naked and vulnerable, their absurdity exposed. This, after all, is the reasoning behind Irigaray's quotations of the masters in *Speculum:* Freud and Plato sound much less impressive in snippets.[33] Like Irigaray, Smith knew the ridiculousness of the lone line. From the *Spectator,* that exemplar of highbrow culture, she cites a laughable excerpt: "Hogs' Puddings—Cornwall's exquisite reply to the continental liver sausage."[34] Smith also undermines the literary hierarchy through the juxtaposition of quotations, revealing the foolishness of both "high" culture and popular culture, or even the hierarchy's potential for collaboration against women's freedom. "Venus . . . quae quoniam rerum naturam sola gubernas" stands close to a passage from a church bulletin:

And here's another dirty one for the Church, from our own correspondence pages: Lonely One. Join a church or a hiking club or a debating society, refuse to spend your evenings along [sic].[35]

The deification of love in high culture appears absurd next to the urgings of the church bulletin, with its misspellings. Smith uses her ability as a coder to recode and thus expose the nonsense of literary hierarchies, which produce similar ideologies on different levels.

Smith also disrupted the linearity of the romance narrative through the insertion of brief fantasies, always escapes from culture into a nature landscape. These fantasies tie Pompey to her matrilineage, since her aunt, a mother figure, is called Auntie Lion, and in a later scene is said to resemble a fish. (Auntie visits the sick Pompey in an outrageous outfit that reminds Pompey of "a mighty fish, very deep and dark and dangerous.")[36] Yet the fantasy nature scenes also tie Pompey to her father, the coder, since they depict prose representations of nature rather than "real" escapes into nature, escapes that, in Pompey's case, prevent her from reaching the romance ending of marriage. Through Pompey, Smith acknowledges the traditions of the mother-line and the father-line, yet confuses them so thoroughly that she herself represents neither tradition, but a complete blend.

Pompey's fantasy departures occur at significant points in the narrative, often where strong-willed Pompey experiences trouble with a controlling boyfriend. The first nature intercut occurs after she and Karl quarrel over the relative merits of German and English culture. Pompey almost immediately escapes Karl and his hierarchial views of culture for her fantasy of a nap in a country haystack. There, nature is very still and quiet; no movement urges her forward in her story. Although a place "outside," the haystack has important relevance to the "inside" of the narrative, since it acts as a wedge in the romance story. Pompey does not give in to Karl, but instead escapes by focusing on her own pleasure and physicality, a movement that completely derails culture. After the haystack moment, Karl's importance to Pompey dissipates, despite his occasional reappearance in the novel.

The most flamboyant of these intercuts occurs when Pompey steps into a Utrillo painting, right after she has a horrifying vision of a fiend holding a carton of ice cream who is strangely like her second boyfriend, Freddy, in that Freddy too offers her sweet pleasures. As Rosalind Coward writes in *Female Desire,* society's pleasures, such as sweet desserts, often distract women from what they are missing: "The pleasure/desire axis appears to be everything women want but it may involve loss—loss of opportunity, loss of freedom, perhaps even loss of happiness."[37] The nightmarish appearance of the fiend portends that Pompey is weakening toward Freddy, and such weakness, which can end only in Pompey's erasure, requires the desperate measure of escape, this time into a Utrillo landscape.

Like her earlier fantasy, her Utrillo escape is one of physical satisfaction. Pompey enters the painting, a landscape of trees, only to find it leads to a crude stone house, hardly representing domesticity or culture. Here Pompey indulges her "hunger" for alternative pleasures:

[T]here is a long oblong dining room with food set out on the dining table. And the food is, first there is grouse *en casserole* and potatoes baked in their jackets, very hot and fresh. And then there is a beer to drink, and then there is mushrooms on toast, and then there is figs fresh picked, and then there is this cool beer to drink.[38]

Significantly, this fantasy is different from the nightmare dream of the fiendish devil holding ice cream. Here there are no sugary sweets, but only nourishment. Rebellious Pompey, expert coder, creates her own fantasy of desire in place of the one cultural convention has handed her: husband as ice cream cone, fulfiller of all one's dreams. After this point, there are only quarrels between Freddy and Pompey.

However, Smith knows that occupying nature's space is only a rhetorical trick, effective temporarily, but nevertheless a trick. One is no more "outside" in this nature than in culture. Smith underscores the nature/culture ambiguity in the fantasies first by using haystacks, reminiscent of Monet paintings, and second by having Pompey literally step into a Utrillo landscape, a painting of nature. Significantly, Pompey's experiences of nature in these two intercuts are all *cultural* representations of nature. In addition, the meal in the stone house of the second fantasy is reminiscent of the sumptuous meal in Virginia Woolf's *A Room of One's Own*. Pompey, through this allusion to Woolf, reminds us that woman's access to the body is always limited and constrained by masculine culture. As Wheeler explains, "[W]e see 'Nature' or 'Society' through the vision and the imagination that aesthetic experience has strengthened and developed in us."[39] For Smith, the problem with lingering too long in nature's territory, as depicted by culture, is that it keeps her and Pompey bound within a binary system. Smith, therefore, never settles long in her nature fantasies.

Smith's retellings, first of *The Bacchae*, later of Tolstoy's *The Live Corpse*, act as other significant interruptions of the novel's romance line. As Wheeler reminds, "The powerful dimension of intertextuality woven into the narrative keeps in play a readerly consciousness of contextuality as essential for participation in the text."[40] The retelling most noted by Smith's critics is that of *The Bacchae*, wedged almost exactly in the center of the novel. Although some readers enjoyed this retelling of the Greek play, many others found it a tedious digression. Indeed, it is a digression, but one that is by no means pointless, since it divides the story of Karl from Freddy, thus hindering the flow of romantic action. In addition, Smith's retelling marks her ability to use patriarchal culture against itself. She "tells" *The Bacchae*, thus revealing that she knows her classics, a sign of the truly educated person. Yet she "retells" *The Bacchae* in a way that undermines, and eventually transforms, its cultural messages.

Rather than depicting the women of Thebes as aligned with the patriarch Pentheus in refusing to worship Dionysus, Smith deletes the women's guilt and allies them with Dionysus:

. . . Pentheus is very stubborn, rather stupid very stubborn. No, he will not recognize the divinity of Dionysus. . . . But the women and Agave they had feelings of forebodings about this sturdy attitude of Pentheus, they thought no good would come of it.

... [A]nd he [Dionysus] now drove the women mad, they were all driven mad, they ran to the mountains with the divine frenzy of madness upon them, and they ran and ran, leaving their husbands and their children. ... [T]hey were so mad and so powerful in their madness.[41]

Smith sees their madness as strength, not as a sign of weakness and torment. Thus, the play becomes a story of revolt against hierarchy and order, rather than Euripides' morality tale of mortals who refuse to honor the gods.

In addition, Smith deletes the last scene of the play, where Agave mourns the death of her son Pentheus, whom she literally dismembered, and acknowledges her guilt. Her retelling ends on a sardonic rather than gruesome note: "Goodbye, shouts Dionysus: Goodbye Pentheus, give my love to Agave. And Pentheus is never seen again alive."[42] Smith's interest in the play is clearly the rebellion of the women through the agency of Dionysus, not their atonement. One has to wonder how much Smith's interpretation of the play was derived from having performed it at North London Collegiate, with its long tradition of rebellious women.[43]

The Bacchae resurfaces in Smith's exposé of popular magazine stories, again acting as a disrupter of ideology, for Smith champions the "mad" women of Thebes against their more docile contemporary counterparts, although their madness is not to be confused with the mad escapades of Pompey or her author. Smith, after all, is the teller of a tale of madness, not one who is truly mad. Smith contrasts the eventual madness of contemporary married women, unable to endure the knowledge that their domestic illusions are not sustainable, with that of the Theban woman, who Smith writes run "excitingly and refreshingly" mad.[44] Although in the play the madness of the Theban women is a sign of Dionysus's power to promote the unnatural and the unfeminine, Smith reads the Greek women's madness as healthy when compared with that of her contemporaries. *The Bacchae*, thus, shows up in two key points in the narrative, provoking her readers, in the interval between romances, to consider the ideological impetus toward romance, as well as its practical drawbacks.

Whereas Smith's retelling of *The Bacchae* functions as an encouragement to rebellion against the stultifying role of wife, Smith's later retelling of Tolstoy's *The Live Corpse* functions as a more general critique of marital relations and the "naturalness" of the romance plot. Pompey uses the play to attack the sanctity of home, relating, as does Tolstoy, the pressures on Lisa and Fedya to conveyors of ideology.[45] Here Smith, through Pompey, reveals that domestic ideology continues across boundaries of genre and time, as Tolstoy's Frau K. is linked to Mrs. Humphry Ward and finally to the popular magazines of Smith's time period:

35

[T]he upshot is Frau K. says that no really nice woman could bring herself to leave her husband. And such a good man too and so nice. And even if he hadn't been, no matter, in fact so much better. . . .

Well to carry on from 'so much the better' which is where Frau K. stopped talking and Pompey took the line, she goes on to say, whatever of Mrs. Haliburton's [sic] troubles there may have been between them, One May Not leave one's husband, but rather One Must Bear One's Cross.

There you are you see, quite simple. If you cannot have your dear husband for a comfort and a delight, for a breadwinner and a cross patch, for a sofa, a chair or a hot-water bottle, one can use him as a Cross to be Borne.

It reminds me of our craft articles published, passim, in all our so-very-much-alike women's papers: How to make a knitting bag out of a top hat. May also be used for a beret or a tea cosy. Free patterns for all included.[46]

Pompey apologizes for digressing from her retelling (in itself a digression), but this apology provokes a reader to question whether her driftings to Mrs. Humphry Ward and popular magazines really are digressions, or rather carefully made connections. After all, Pompey sides with Fedya, who runs away to a gypsy camp to escape marriage.[47] What Pompey shows is that many cultural forms speak in similar voices and send similar domestic messages.

Finally, the retelling itself acts as a means of denying the closure of the novel, since Smith literally tacks on Tolstoy. The Tolstoy displaces or replaces the end of her novel, leaving it without a solution to the Pompey and Freddy question. To further complicate the situation, Pompey cannot finish her Tolstoy retelling, as she admits she hasn't finished reading the play and does not intend to. Thus, Pompey champions both writing and reading without access to endings.

In crossing the romance with these narrative interruptions, Smith reminds her readers of the coercive quality of domestic ideology, but also of women's ability to recode their culture. Smith suggests, paradoxically, that the only way "out" of culture is through culture. To ignore the multiple forms of cultural representation promoting domesticity is to ignore the very real effect it has on women readers, but "paying attention" to domestic ideology need not necessarily reproduce domestic ideology intact, as *Novel* reveals. Smith's attempts at decoding and recoding were to continue in *Over the Frontier,* which also tells Pompey's story.

CONTINUING THE ASSAULT: *OVER THE FRONTIER*

One of Smith's most baffling intercuts in Pompey's two-novel narrative is the fantasy war adventure at the end of *Over the Frontier* (1938). After a series of party sequences in the mode of *Novel,* the story suddenly, and most disturbingly, vaults into a Kafkaesque plot of war and intrigue. As might be expected, reviewers of the 1938 edition and the 1980 Virago/1982 Pinnacle reprint were hard-pressed to make any sense out of this abrupt plot and genre shift. Those who felt the most warmth toward Smith and Pompey questioned rather than criticized, as did Marie Scott-James in her February 1938 review for the *London Mercury:* "Is it [the end of her book] an enterprise against Fascism, against the tyranny of ambition and pride, against dictatorship in whatever form?"[48] Smith's more critical readers, such as Joyce Carol Oates in her 1982 review marking the American reprints, found this shift to be a major flaw: "*Over the Frontier* . . . shifts, surprisingly and I'm afraid not altogether plausibly, to an adventure-espionage tale. . . ."[49] Even Victoria Glendinning, who expresses a fuller understanding of the novel than most, is not entirely sure she has "got" the ending: "The cold night-rides and the code-messages and Pompey's ruthless efficiency have all, surely, been a dream: A sort of a joke."[50] Contemporary reviewers Jack Barbera and William McBrien conclude that "[t]he novel is not finally a success, in part because of the jarring shift mid-book from realism to surrealism."[51]

What these reviewers demonstrate is that the novel is impossible to read, almost unintelligible in fact, without a cultural framework informed by gender. The shift in the middle of *Frontier* is hardly an arbitrary one; it marks a move from the "feminine" genre of the romance plot to the "masculine" genre of the adventure story. Anyone questioning the stories assigned to the feminine gender would eventually need to encounter and question those assigned to the masculine. The two stories in *Frontier*, romance and adventure, are therefore not unlinked; they are complementary stories provided by a culture that strongly differentiates masculine and feminine roles. Neither is the shift unmotivated. Pompey's loss of a future with Freddy has caused her to become increasingly ill, to the point that she is in grave danger of descending into the romance plot's dysphoric ending, death.[52]

Although it is 1938, the novel opens with Pompey suffering from what appears to be a famous Victorian ailment, another clue that links the story back to its Victorian predecessors. Pompey is frequently listless and depressed, not at all like the exuberant Pompey of the first novel. Her symptoms greatly resemble those of the neurasthenic, as described by George Savage, Virginia Woolf's one-time doctor:

A woman, generally single, or in some way not in a condition for performing her reproductive function, having suffered from some real or imagined trouble, or having passed through a phase of hypochondriasis of sexual character, and often being of a highly nervous stock, becomes the interesting invalid.[53]

Although intended as medical description, Savage's diagnosis really exposes the narrative prescriptivity of Victorian society: If a woman is unable to fulfill her normal social function as wife and mother, then she becomes an "interesting invalid."

It is Savage's narrative, reflective of social narrative, that Pompey's story parodies, revealing its absurdity. Like her Victorian predecessors, Pompey succumbs to nervous illness after refusing her only suitor, but her comic exaggeration undermines her plight:

Several weeks running into months now I have been sick again, I am suffering from the chic Victorian complaint of swooning and the vapours, but I have not yet come to chewing blotting-paper as the anaemic girls of that time did, quires of pink blotting-paper between meals. I imagine them getting together slyly in the rainswept gardens under the rose trees of an evening in July. How many sheets of blotting-paper dear Amelia, well that is good but not so good as Edwina. . . .[54]

By connecting her illness to these nineteenth-century women, Pompey lets her readers know that her condition is as much social as psychological, imposed by those who make illness a fashionable competition among women.

While conveying the absurdity of Savage's social prescriptions, Pompey's narrative also reveals their dark side: just because women are aware of the socially determined nature of their acts does not mean that they are necessarily able to avoid them. Exuberant Pompey appears set on her determined course, death. Despite her understanding of her situation, she claims that "[n]ow my whole life is about to end."[55] Well-intentioned friends, such as Josephine, push her toward death, by emphasizing her sadness, even though Pompey knows this is an oversimplification of her feelings:

[T]his strong and forceful Josephine has created her picture of Pompey, and has for the moment projected it upon my vision, so that I forget the gay light moments, and the raffish black and hateful demon that runs alongside, and think only of this pure element of sadness that is quiet and touching and in its quality eternal.[56]

Standing on the cliffs at Josephine's, feeling the pull of "delicious abandonment to elemental disturbance," Pompey eventually considers killing herself.[57]

Although finally able to escape death, Pompey is nevertheless trapped in a repetitive loop: her reentry into society entails rest, cure, and future romance. Society intends, and almost succeeds, in "curing" Pompey of her illness. Without a protest, she allows herself to be sent off on a rest cure, which according to Elaine Showalter was the traditional treatment for neurasthenia.[58] Her doctors seem unaware that the nineteenth century is over:

"You must have a complete change of scene. And a long rest. Far from towns. Near the sea. Close to the best medical opinion. If possible with pinewoods in the vicinity."[59]

Influenced by the doctor's authority, Pompey obeys and goes off to the sanatorium of Schloss Tilssen, only to face the traditional fate of the nineteenth-century patient, boredom. As Elaine Showalter explains, nineteenth-century doctors realized that their patients frequently became so bored with the rest cure that they often proclaimed themselves cured after a time.[60] Regaled with Josephine's boring gossip, Pompey, as did so many nineteenth-century patients, decides she is fat enough and cured, ready to embark upon another romance, this time with the "hale and hearty" Tom Satterthwaite. It looks as though Pompey is about to be pulled into the romance plot yet again.

But Smith's imagination calls a halt to this endless cycle of repetition, which can end only in marriage, an option that Pompey refuses to accept. Pompey finds herself thrown into the other gender and another story, an adventure, since it offers the only well-worn cultural alternative to the story of femininity. Thus, the adventure story, like the narrative intrusions in *Novel*, serves as an intercut, or a disruption of the romance plot, this time between Pompey and Tom Satterthwaite.

The adventure story ending of *Frontier* becomes an exploration of masculine narratives and the possibilities they offer to women writers who have tired of the restrictions of femininity. Masculinity and its character were also the subject of Woolf's 1938 essay *Three Guineas*, and although neither Woolf nor Smith could have read the other's work, they were preoccupied with the same questions. What roles are available for rebellious women to follow? Is there any advantage to them in adopting the masculine role? *Frontier* can be read, in effect, as an amicable dialogue with Woolf: Smith agrees with Woolf's opinion in *Three Guineas* that masculinity, as currently constructed, is dangerous, because its values are separatist and hierarchical. While its values might be advantageous to individual women, they are not advantageous to society as a whole.

Three Guineas paints a picture of society as historically divided by its different roles for men and women. According to Woolf, divisions in the private sphere lead to those in the public, ultimately creating a society based on paradigms of dominance and submission. The quest for dominance generates a hierarchical society, where men distinguish themselves through their uniforms, their titles, and their ceremonies. Such seemingly innocuous tokens of difference are truly sinister for Woolf, since she argues that society's hierarchical mechanisms necessarily lead to war and violence. Woolf sees the masculine gender and its institutions as inevitably linked to a quest for power and dominance. She only hopes that women, because of their different historic vantage point, will be able to disrupt old patterns:

[W]e can refuse all such distinctions and all such uniforms for ourselves. This would be a slight but definite contribution to the problem before us—how to prevent war; and one that a different training and a different tradition put more easily within our reach than within yours.[61]

According to Woolf, women's "different tradition" might enable them to reconfigure society, as is evidenced by Woolf's fantasies of a different educational system and a new world order without violence.

Although Smith is more skeptical than Woolf about women's ability to act as saviors to their society, her understanding of masculinity as hierarchical and violent is close to Woolf's. Additionally, Woolf and Smith share the same method, ironic retelling, to get their point across. Woolf mimics male critics in her imaginary letters, while Pompey herself acts as a retelling of masculinity, in donning one of those uniforms that Woolf warns against. Through comic technique, they expose the very real, and not so comic, horrors created by a divided gender system.

Once Pompey has crossed the frontier, a border that is associated with gender as well as with national boundaries, she begins to change in significant ways. At first, she is irritated by her masculine uniform, sign of her gender switch: "Oh this coat. Oh it is so detestable. And the thoughts that go with it, they are so utterly detestable."[62] But slowly she becomes accustomed to the privileges and grows to like the responsibility, despite signs that her character is becoming progressively darker.

In her private life, she grows competitive with her former fiancé, Tom Satterthwaite. Once her leader, he finds her slowly becoming his. Their relationship weakens: "No longer do we have our laughing quick happy days and nights together, no longer am I to be cajoled, informed, delighted."[63] Smith exposes that relationships based on gender distinction necessarily require difference and subsequently the subordination of one partner. As Pompey becomes increasingly masculine, Tom must start becoming increasingly feminine. Pompey frets, "And as I grow stronger Tom grows weaker, on occasion petulant, frivolous, irrational, and obstinate."[64] Someone, after all, has to act the woman in a heterosexual couple, although this gender shift exposes the ridiculousness of such a pattern.

Pompey's desires to dominate in the private sphere extend to the public sphere, where she grows eager to take Tom's job. She enjoys her successes, finding them strangely exhilarating, a break from her former life. The male hierarchy of this fantasy world, represented by Generalissimo Clever-Pie and the Archbishop, insures the continuance of its power structure by urging her on, promising her a promotion. Pompey eventually kills a man on her way up the careerist ladder, but she does not care. As did the propagandists in World War I, she subordinates the enemy, devaluing his life by turning him into an animal, a Rat-face.[65]

The greatest difference between Woolf and Smith is that Smith finds women complicit in the hierarchical system, whereas Woolf gives them the privileged position of outsider. Woolf's *Three Guineas* is written from the premise that women are less likely to become masculinized because they have been steeped in different social traditions. Smith fears, however, that it is precisely women's role as outsiders that makes them vulnerable. They risk being corrupted because their experience of substantial power is new, and, therefore, infinitely attractive. Pompey recalls an incident in a tea shop, where a group of waitresses, subordinates, mistreat a gathering of elderly, rich ladies. Far from condemning the incident, Harriet and Pompey watch the entire scene with glee.[66] Smith does not tie this scene into the rest of the narrative, but it would seem to be an acknowledgment of the lower echelon's desire for power. Oppression, Smith suggests, often only recycles itself.

Smith does hope, however, that there is a way out of the oppositional logic of the gender system, which assigns women to one narrative and men to another. Her final answer would seem to be that one must take on the role of the exuberant Mrs. Pouncer, a double agent and an expert coder. Not trusted by male spies, Mrs. Pouncer seems to be playing a game that has nothing to do with the war over the border, or the hierarchical advancement games of Generalissimo Clever-Pie and the Archbishop. Tom Satterthwaite says of her: "Oh yes, she's in it, . . . she is very decidedly in it, but on which side, on which side?"[67] And Pompey's friend Josephine declares that Pompey has a "really vicious passion for this old girl."[68] Through the character of Mrs. Pouncer, Smith promotes shifting identities and allegiances. For Smith, to remain settled is to allow one's capture, not by any elusive enemy but by "one's own side."

Having explored, as well as destroyed, the narratives of both romance and adventure, Pompey is left, after *Frontier,* with nowhere to go. Able to exist in neither feminine nor masculine garb, Pompey self-destructs, only to be replaced with Celia in *The Holiday.* Celia attempts what Pompey has not been able to, to create a world "outside" the gendered narratives of Smith's period. As did Smith's foremothers, Richardson and Woolf, Smith was to turn to alternative rhythms, what Smith herself called, in *Novel,* the "rhythm of friendship."[69] Pompey, caught between the rhythm of friendship and the rhythm of romance, was unable to completely enact a narrative based on friendship. Celia, however, who is as much Pompey's alter ego as Smith's, does manage almost entirely to pull herself out of the rhythm of romance.

MOVING BEYOND THE ROMANCE:
THE RHYTHM OF FRIENDSHIP IN *THE HOLIDAY*

Smith's third novel, *The Holiday,* suggests that changing narrative, as well as changing society, ultimately involves moving away from old patterns and creating new ones. Interestingly, such an answer is the one Woolf came to in *The Years* (1937), whose structure is based on patterns of friendship, like that of *The Holiday.* Although Woolf presents the female outsider as the answer to changing society in *Three Guineas,* at least in this one work she agrees with Smith that the entire gender system must be dismantled. While *Frontier* created a dialogue with Woolf's *Three Guineas* over the destructiveness of masculinity and the divided gender system, *The Holiday* and *The Years* discuss the possibility of creating new world orders out of new narratives.

As in the dialogue between *Frontier* and *Three Guineas,* it is Woolf who is the visionary optimist, while Smith remains more realistic and finally more despairing. Perhaps such a difference can be attributed to Woolf's having witnessed a period in which feminism actually triumphed, whereas Smith lived through a downturn in women's rights. Although Smith's Celia does not see herself vis-à-vis the movement of feminism, she does see herself as a postrevolutionary: "[I] like better the time that is more crucial than revolution, that is the time when revolution succeeds and must govern."[70] Woolf, on the other hand, is always the classic revolutionary, envisioning new ground, new places. Perhaps such a difference can also be read as a function of their different class positions. Smith asserts, through Celia, that the lower middle class are necessarily more pragmatic in their visions:

The free-blowing revolutionaries, the classless artists, these are the salt of the earth, for they have the power to see a thing while it is yet a long way off. But you cannot make a diet of salt, and it is through the use and practice of the middle-classes that the vision is made actual. I have not found the middle-classes against the new ideas, so much as anxious how they may be applied; but of course I am speaking of the less wealthy sort of middle-class person, such as we have at home.[71]

Contrary to Marx, Smith does not believe the middle class to be hopelessly wedded to the status quo, though she does link revolutionary understanding with the "less wealthy sort of middle-class person."

Woolf's *The Years* focuses on the evolutionary nature of progress and thus remains somewhat Victorian, despite its destruction of the family unit. Eleanor, one of four sisters born in a Victorian household, is a firm believer in a "new world," in living with people differently, i.e., not in family units. More confused and less grandiose in their rhetoric, her niece and nephew, Peggy and North, nevertheless catch her meaning in glimmers. Through her chronicling of three generations—Victorian, Edwardian, and modern—Woolf portrays that the world is changing its understanding of human relations. Hers is a novel of shifting friendships, among both distant relations and the unrelated, like the homosexual Nicholas Brown.[72]

Like Woolf's, Smith's novel is literally a holiday from the world as we know it. Smith's change to the name Celia, which stands for heavenly, marks the entry into another world. However, this world has little of the ecstatic joy of a utopia: *The Holiday* is a novel of sadness and pain, for Smith believes that change does not come without pain. Unlike Eleanor from *The Years*, who cannot wait for change, which she connects with a gloriously beautiful dawn, Smith's characters drag their feet, longing for an easier path.

That a new world is badly needed is made clear immediately in *The Holiday,* which tells the story of the postwar era, one that has learned little from the previous war. Of course, Smith wrote the novel during the war, but the ease with which she changed the novel to its post-World War II setting is telling. Dominating nations still strive to keep others in their subordinate places. America and Russia have replaced Britain's power, but other than that, the world is still remarkably similar to the world at war. The same power constructs, based on difference, are still in place.

A world that emphasizes differences, and organizes them hierarchically, must necessarily produce nationalism and imperialism, for both occur through a sense that the Other is different and necessarily inferior to the Self. Smith's preoccupation in *The Holiday* is similar to Edward Said's in *Orientalism:* "Can one divide human reality, as indeed human reality seems to be genuinely divided, into clearly different cultures, histories, traditions, societies, even races, and survive the consequences humanly?"[73] Smith has no more of a definitive answer to these questions than Said, but her position on nationalism is made clear through Celia. At the beginning of *The Holiday,* Celia claims: "I hate the petty nationalismus idea, I said, this idea will be the death of the Peace, when the postwar is over and Peace comes, you will see it will be the death of it."[74]

Unlike Said, though, Smith draws a connection between sexual division and political structuring, between the family romance and the political. It is the desire for the Other, bred of the sense of difference in the family, that leads to the need to possess. As Gilles Deleuze and Felix Guattari have theorized, channeled desire colonizes, and in turn leads to further colonization: "Oedipus is always colonization pursued by other means, it is the interior colony, and we shall see that even here, at home, where we Europeans are concerned, it is our intimate colonial education."[75] Just as the lover desires his beloved, Celia desires India. Remembering her happy childhood there, Celia realizes that relinquishing possession of India is like losing a beloved: "So this is the other side of the question, of the famous old-bogey question of England-in-India, yes this is the other side of that. And how can we leave India when we have these loving memories, how can we do it?"[76] To change the world, Smith suggests, one must start not at the top but at the psychological bottom: One must escape from a world fundamentally structured on sameness and difference.

Sameness is as much a trap as difference. Celia's relationship with her aunt would seem to be a replaying of the pre-oedipal, an escape from patriarchy through the bonds of mother and daughter:

[M]ost women, especially in the lower and lower-middle classes, are conditioned early to having "father" the centre of the home-life, with father's chair and father's dinner, and father's *Times* and father says, so they are not brought up like me to be this wicked selfish creature, to have no boring old father-talk, to have no papa at all that one attends to, to have a darling Aunt to come home to, that one admires, that is strong, happy, simple, shrewd, staunch, loving, upright and bossy. . . .[77]

But Celia declares her relation with her aunt to be an in-between relationship, not one of sameness, by insisting upon the removed relation: Auntie is not her mother. Society, as it does frequently, tries to simplify the relationship between Celia and Auntie; the butcher, for example, insists upon seeing Auntie as mother.[78] But Smith suggests that the aunt does not and cannot represent the utopian lapse into the mother. There are always tensions with Auntie: "I love my Aunt, my Aunt loves me. There is this straining and anxiety in love between dear relations. . . ."[79] Not content to stay home with Auntie, Celia must journey out to other connections.

The "others" consist of her many friends and, particularly, her two cousins, Tom and Caz. Like Woolf in *The Years,* Smith sees relationships between cousins as a metaphor for an alternative relationship with the world: they represent neither the intimate bonds of one's immediate family, nor the removed distance of strangers. However, Smith recognizes that any relationship can end up replaying the familial, since the desire for possession is continually strong. Society pushes the individual into the roles of the past: Celia's uncle would like to see her marry her cousin Tom. Celia resists, but still feels the pain of separation from Tom: "And I think of Tom, of my uncle's mad son Tom, and wish for comfort I was in his arms again, and much comfort that should be, it is not in Tom's arms that comfort lies. In whose arms, then, in whose arms may comfort lie, is it permitted?"[80] As Celia comes to realize, there finally is no permanent comfort.

Her relationship with her other cousin, Caz, is a more hopeful one, since he represents an alternative from patterns of sameness and difference. Theirs is a relationship based on friendship rather than romance.[81] However, such a relationship is difficult to maintain, because there is always the temptation to make the relationship more than it really is. Celia finds herself content and not content at the same time:

How happy I felt now, lying beside my beloved wise cousin, my solemn friend. Why do I fret and cry because he can be nothing else than a friend? Was he not always my true friend, and is he not this now? It is sufficient to lie beside him in friendship and agreement. His thoughts and words run with mine.[82]

Although Celia sometimes longs for Tom and the possessive relationship he represents, she ultimately prefers her free but insecure life with Caz. As Caz suggests, romance cannot be the answer for them: "You must not be romantic about Tom, you must not suppose there is a solution there, there is no solution for us and no answer."[83]

The world of Caz, emblem of shifting connections, is a scary one, but it nevertheless keeps Celia from the world of exchange. Celia distrusts her female friends who urge marriage upon her and hide its possessive qualities:

And they are at first immensely pleased about this that I have been saying, but then they begin to wish not to stress how martyr-like wonderful it is, and they begin to say how much one is missing if one does not have it. . . .[84]

Celia knows she cannot marry in this society because she would be literally used up. She longs for a redefinition of marriage, a kind of joyful polygamy: "I could never marry because of fear, I should like to have one-third of a man, to be the third wife, perhaps, with her own house. . . ."[85] But she realizes this arrangement is hardly possible.

In rejecting romance with her cousins Tom and Caz, Celia frees herself from both the socially acceptable desire of marriage and the less accepted, but nevertheless culturally generated, channel of incest. As Gilles Deleuze and Felix Guattari have explained, the culture represses by channeling the explosive, revolutionary force of desire into a desire *for* something: "Oedipal desires are the bait, the disfigured image by means of which repression catches desire in the trap."[86] Celia and Caz do not succumb to their incestuous desires, unlike Celia's father and Caz's mother, because they recognize that transgressing the taboo of incest is just another trap. Hardly a rebellious act, incest only affirms society's oedipal power by coding or channeling the nature of rebellion: "[T]he incestuous drives are the disfigured image of the repressed."[87] Rejecting oedipal law involves a recognition that its binary system of choice—obey or rebel—is really a nonchoice. Perhaps a better choice, the rhythm of friendship is at least one alternative to oedipal law.

The central metaphor of *The Holiday*, always a favorite of Smith's, is travel, her concrete representation of the "rhythm of friendship." Repeating the horse motif from the first two novels, Smith has Caz and Pompey ride away from "the best day of the holiday" on the same horse, Noble. Yet it is not only their metaphor, but, everyone else's. The railway station, representation of the shifting interconnections of people, is another fundamental image of *The Holiday*. Caz remarks:

Life is like a railway station . . . the train of birth brings us in, the train of death will carry us away, and meanwhile we are cooling our heels upon the platform and waiting for the connection, and stamping up and down the platform, and passing the time of day with the other people who are also waiting.[88]

Smith's new world order is more mundane, with its people stamping their feet, than Eleanor's visionary dawn in *The Years*, but it is no less revolutionary in its demand that we rethink the most basic structures of society.

Strangely, Smith's most utopian novel is also her least certain, and her most tearful. She is not at all sure that human beings can live without continually attempting to possess others. Although Celia maintains an uneasy balance in her relationships between Tom and Caz, she continually desires more, that close connection of marriage and the fulfillment that comes from home. Nor is she hopeful that attempts on the public front to curb this possessiveness, manifested in nationalism, will be any more successful:

[W]hen I think of England, my dear country, I think with pride, aggression and complacency. I tie up my own pride and advantage with England's, I have no integrity, no honesty, no generous idea of a better way of life than that way which gives cream to England. But where can one get this idea of a new world, and how can one believe it?[89]

We do not know at the end of the novel if Celia will go back to her intelligence agency coding job or whether Caz will join his regiment in India. If they do, they will only continue their involvement in a hierarchical and imperialist world order. But Uncle Heber's escapist, Christian retreat offers no answers either. Predictably, Smith closes the novel without any closure, as her characters are literally at a dead end.

Although Celia herself never achieves certainty, Smith's novels suggest that rewriting traditional narratives and envisioning divergent ones are at least one possible way of obtaining a "new world." Smith's most exciting characters, Pompey and Celia, but also others like Harriet and Mrs. Pouncer, are "coders." Smith places her faith not in any one vision of the future but in the coding ability itself.

3

Poems and Drawings

1937–1966

One of the many folders in the Stevie Smith archive at the University of Tulsa is filled with dozens of her drawings, small, awkward sketches on scraps of notepaper no bigger than two or three inches. A handful reveals characteristic Smith subjects: a young girl with a hair bow, a woman with an extravagantly large hat, and an animal or two. Smith never used many of the drawings in this particular folder to illustrate her poetry, but at least a few were reproduced, first in the original volumes, later in her *Collected Poems*. The unimpressiveness of Smith's drawings, made clearer by their appearance in the original, would only seem to support the conclusion of many of her contemporaries, that the amateurish quality of the drawings detracts from the excellence of the poetry. Philip Larkin, an early Smith supporter, wrote that the drawings possessed "an amateurishness reminiscent of Lear, Waugh, and Thurber without much compensating felicity."[1] Critic and poet Jonathan Williams went so far as to wish that her "memo pads [with the drawings] had disappeared into the fire."[2] Unlike Smith herself, contemporary poets, critics, and publishers often felt that her use of the drawings was an unfortunate mistake.

Because of this early reception, the recognition of Smith's poems and drawings as a composite art form has been delayed. Not until the work of Jack Barbera and William McBrien in the mid-1980s did Smith's drawings, or the conditions under which they were created, receive more than a cursory comment. Barbera and McBrien document the risks Smith took to publish her drawings with her poems, in the process almost failing to find a publisher for her now most famous volume, *Not Waving but Drowning* (1957).[3] They suggest that Smith's drawings are often relevant to the poetry, frequently adding layers of meaning that previously went unnoticed.[4] Most significantly, they point out that the New Critical construct under which Smith's poems and drawings were evaluated in the fifties and the following two decades is completely inadequate for dealing with an illustrated poetry.[5] Yet they conclude their groundbreaking discussion of her artwork with a surprisingly dismissive comment: "[I]t is clear that in the overwhelming majority of cases the drawings are mainly decorative."[6]

More recent critics of Smith's poetry, such as Sheryl Stevenson and Romana Huk, have tended to read the drawings as an extension of the text, without acknowledging the drawings *as* drawings.[7] That is, they do not see them as a separate art form with a separate cultural history. Such an omission is somewhat surprising, given the considerable body of work on Smith's poetic and artistic ancestors, William Blake and Edward Lear, that takes precisely this approach. For example, W. J. T. Mitchell claims that Blake's "composite art is . . . an interaction between two vigorously independent modes of expression."[8] Despite the fact that some of the most interesting critics of Smith have used Bakhtinian theory to emphasize the dialogic nature of her work, none have yet examined the dialogue occurring between Smith's composite art form and other cultural discourses, both verbal and visual.

In fact, Smith's graphics are crucial to her art, not mere decoration. She used the artistic tradition of Blake and Lear to contest the negative imagery of women so prevalent in the interwar and post-World War II periods.[9] Smith felt that women often suffered from a loss of energy and vitality in the traditional marriage, and her work seeks to offer alternative possibilities, among them remaining single. Her work most directly confronts the interwar image of the unhappy spinster, a hapless and hopeless victim of the (illusory) numerical imbalance between men and women after the war. Although Smith's published composite art spans a period of twenty-five years, it frequently refers back to this dialogue. As many of the arguments for the return to traditional gender roles were advanced both after World War I and after World War II, the continuity in Smith's work is hardly surprising. In questioning these traditional gender roles through a mixed media art form, her work anticipates that of feminist artists in the seventies and eighties, such as Britain's Mary Kelly, who, like Smith, mixed art forms in an attempt to undo the appealing coherency of woman's image in mass cultural products.

Since Smith was largely unable to place her drawings in her last, posthumous volume, *Scorpion,* this chapter will focus on the poems and drawings in her first five volumes (through 1957) and two later volumes of selected poems that include original work with drawings, *Selected Poems* (1962) and *The Frog Prince* (1966). As Smith did sometimes move her drawings, it is important to refer to both the original volume and *Collected Poems*. Drawings discussed occur in both the original volume and *Collected Poems*, unless otherwise stated.

Reviewers and critics, as well as Smith herself, have traced her work to the composite art tradition of Blake and Lear, yet no one has examined what, exactly, Smith shares with her forefathers, since in many respects these artists' specific techniques and interests are dissimilar. Here the considerable criticism on Blake's and Lear's composite art proves helpful, first in comparing artistic techniques, then in examining what kind of art, and audience, these techniques demand. Smith shared at least two crucial stylistic traits with her forefathers: Her drawings employ their antirepresentational style, in which images float almost without background, and their counterpointing of visual and verbal representation. These shared characteristics have the effect of creating a demanding art that relies on an active reader/viewer to pull together disparate visual images and verbal constructs. Despite their dates and varying political backgrounds, Blake, Lear, and Smith are similarly interested in mixing media and discourses, bridging popular and high culture, and closing the breach between creator and audience. Like Brecht and many postmodernist artists, their composite art works to "achiev[e] a different form of realist knowledge" by "actively involving the spectator in its production and its translation into action."[10]

One of the startling traits of Blake, Lear, and Smith's visual art is its puzzling nature, given its apparent straightforward simplicity. Their art appears accessible in its reproduction of recognizable human beings, and yet it is finally what W. J. T. Mitchell calls "anti-pictorial" or "symbolic" rather than "representational," because its figures act as "emblems," often mysterious emblems, since they are surrounded by white space.[11] Paradoxically, this emblematic, collagelike art is a particularly powerful political art form, since it requires its readers to make meaning through the connection between the art work and other cultural discourses. Once activated by a reader/viewer, it begins to question and undermine other, more dominant discourses in the culture, particularly those maintaining traditional hierarchic distinctions of class, gender, and national origin or ethnic background.

It is exactly this emblematic nature of Smith's work that her early reviewers misunderstood. Their reasoning seems to have been that an art that cares about representation should therefore be representational. Such a criterion occasionally seems to have rubbed off on Smith herself, since at least once she bemoaned her inability to "reproduce" hands and feet.[12] But what is valuable about Smith's art is its emblematic nature. When we look at her many illustrations of women, we see not women as photographed in women's magazines but cultural *signs* of womanhood. Her drawings comment on the way women exist as cultural emblems of femininity, not as they "really are," since women's existence is at least partially dependent on interaction with these emblems.

Equally important to understanding the composite art of Smith is the way in which her poems and drawings often work at "counterpoint" with each other, as do many of the composite artworks in Blake's and Lear's canons. Smith's drawings are not illustrations in the traditional sense, meaning that they are not, as Lisa Ede has said of Lear's work, "appendages to the word, slavish visual imitations or recreations of a literary event."[13] Throughout their analysis of Smith's poems and drawings, Barbera and McBrien use the word *mirroring* to describe the relationship between poem and drawing, thus suggesting that poem and drawing merely reflect each other.[14] However, it is clear that they have a more complex relation in mind, since they conclude by generalizing that the drawings act in "harmony" with and "counterpoint" to each other, "counterpoint" suggesting a more dialogic approach to Smith's drawings than "mirroring."[15] Although Smith's drawings occasionally do "harmonize" with the poems, it is far more common for the poems and drawings to be decidedly out of sync with each other.

Following in this tradition of counterpoint, Smith's art acts as a kind of cultural remix. Like those children's books that combine the head of a hippopotamus with the body of a mouse, Smith's poems and drawings recombine the images of femininity in her time period, or combine contemporary imagery with that from past discourses. The cultural dissonance of her composite art is intensified by frequent juxtapositions between "high" and "low" art. A poetic reference to Turner stands next to a popular magazine image; a crudely drawn spinster is juxtaposed with a poem based on a church hymn. Like the more explicitly feminist artists who followed her, Smith's art recreates through recycling. As Craig Owens has noted in his discussion of contemporary feminist artists,

Most of these artists . . . work with the existing repertory of cultural imagery— not because they either lack originality or criticize it—but because their subject, feminine sexuality, is always constituted in and as representation, a representation of difference.[16]

For Smith, the only way to combat traditional femininity is to underline its representations, thereby making her reader/viewer aware of the contradictory and conflicting signals that only appear coherent.

Because of Smith's subject matter, a comparison with Blake and Lear can go only so far, since making a statement on femininity was not the *primary* focus of Blake's and Lear's art, as it often is with Smith's. At this point, a comparison with the feminist mixed media artists of the seventies and eighties, especially her later compatriot Mary Kelly, is useful. If Blake and Lear taught Smith a particularly dialogic art, then a comparison with Kelly reveals how she used this dialogic art to undermine the unity and coherency of feminine representation.

At first, such a comparison appears far-fetched, since Kelly's recent perspex triptychs would seem to be far afield from Smith's more simplistic poems and line drawings. The two share nothing in terms of actual artistic materials, but they do share a compulsion to work across boundaries by mixing visual and verbal symbols. Kelly's 1985 work *Corpus,* with its mixture of fashion shots and handwritten texts, oddly resembles Smith's poems and drawings in its attempt to pit verbal and visual representations of women against each other. Not only do the women artists mix media, but they also mix disparate discourses. In Kelly's work, according to Pollock, "[f]ashion plates, anatomy and popular medical discourse, romantic fiction are selected and reworked."[17] Smith too employs a wide variety of discourses: references to fairy tales and folklore combine with those from newspapers and popular magazines. Smith's and Kelly's work always presents a fractured, nonunified image, one that purposefully transgresses the cultural boundaries limiting women.

Smith's art of disunity resembles that of contemporary feminist visual artists in its attempt to deconstruct the coherency of dominant images of womanhood through a mixture of competing art forms. According to Pollock, "re"vision is necessarily the goal of the feminist artist:

The pleasures of which feminists have of necessity been sceptical are those involved in the hypostasized image and those involved in narrative itself. The one promises fullness and wholeness, the palpable simplicity of visible truth . . . the other secures the viewer/reader within a singular flow of interrelating and mutually reinforcing meanings and positions.[18]

Smith's and Kelly's fractured, multilayered art undoes the plastic coherence of womanhood presented in mass cultural products such as women's magazines. Whereas Kelly attacks the glossy fashion photos of contemporary culture, Smith's artwork can be read as a response to the line drawings that illustrated women's magazines when she first started working at Pearson's in the early twenties.

Smith's and Kelly's mixing of art forms prevents the reader/viewer from lapsing into the fetishism of the masculine gaze, and thus creates a different relationship between artist and viewer. According to Griselda Pollock, disrupting coherency is necessary in order to create a new viewer:

If the dominant pacification of populations takes place through passive consumption of meanings naturalized through realist modes of representation, feminist critical practice must resist such specularity especially when the visible object par excellence is the image of woman. It has to create an entirely new kind of spectator as part and parcel of its representational strategies.[19]

By counterpointing different media and different discourses, Smith and Kelly create a disruptive art that unravels not only cultural imagery per se, as in Blake and Lear, but particularly the patriarchal image of woman, who has always stood, as Pollock mentions above, as the "visible object par excellence."

But as much as comparisons are useful in elucidating both Smith's technique and her relationship to an audience, such comparisons are finally limited, since each writer/artist works in a specific period, with specific techniques and materials. As Andreas Huyssen asserts, "Resistance will always have to be specific and contingent upon the cultural field within which it operates."[20] When Smith started working at Pearson's in 1923, color gravure, the process that creates glossy fashion photos, had not yet been invented. The women's magazines produced by Pearson's, later Newnes, Pearson, were then largely illustrated with line drawings. From an examination of these interwar magazines in the British Library, it would seem that the line drawings served much the same function as the glossy photos in contemporary magazines. According to Janice Winship, women's magazines create their coherent imagery of women through a differential use of verbal and visual imagery, the visual imagery often carrying the fantasy or ideal aspect of womanhood.[21] That Smith was aware of the enticing nature of magazine visuals is made clear in *Novel on Yellow Paper,* where Pompey critiques the "superior fashion paper" for giving "nice clothes to its readers and gilt-edged ideas all ready to try on."[22] Her connection between the clothes, as depicted visually, and the ideas, which like the clothes can be tried on, suggests that the visuals can be transformed into ideas and ideas into practice.

Smith's painfully awkward drawings prove a startling contrast to these polished, romantic depictions of womanhood in women's magazines. Smith's composite art works to destabilize, and therefore deconstruct, the ideal feminine images of her time by mixing them with her culture's less ideal images and images from past "high" art and popular discourses. As mentioned in chapter 1, traditional femininity was making a comeback in mass media culture when Smith began working for Pearson's: women were expected to give up newfound jobs to returning soldiers and take up their traditional role as homemakers and childbearers. Since working-class women were no longer as willing to work as domes-

53

tics, middle-class women were needed to do necessary housework. In response to this need, the mass media culture created the scientific housewife, the woman who could be proud of her "professional" role in the home.[23] Shiny new appliances, smaller versions of those used in hotels, supposedly made her work less difficult. But, as Dolores Hayden points out, "these inventions eroded the autonomy of women at least as much as they contributed to saving women's labor."[24] In addition, standards of cleanliness increased, leaving women's household hours unchanged.[25] Because the birthrate had fallen dramatically, and because of war losses, the "new" housewife was also under pressure to bear children. Motherhood, always connected with femininity, nevertheless achieved a new, specific meaning, and urgency, in the interwar years.[26] Eugenics (and eventually fascism) promoted the "production" of healthy babies for the good of the nation.[27] Even feminism, under the supposedly "new" feminists, championed motherhood, hardly questioning the traditional sex role system.[28]

Any woman who threatened to disrupt this new order was catalogued as marginal, if not freakish. The infamous flappers, whose love of pleasure, particularly sexual pleasure without motherhood, was seen as dangerous.[29] But even more germaine to Smith's art was the notion of the superfluous women. The war had supposedly created a superfluity of women for whom no mate would be found, although Martin Pugh points out that an actual imbalance between men and women never really existed because of the halt of male emigration.[30] More likely, the "superfluous" designation resulted from the single woman's connection to militant feminism, and, subsequently, society's attempt to control "deviant" women.[31] Unmarried women who had formerly seen themselves as socially useful were increasingly cast as marginal, abnormal figures. Influenced by sexologists who promoted the healthy "naturalness" of sex, society's views of the unmarried woman gradually changed from 1910 to 1940. The word "spinster," originally a neutral term for an unmarried woman, took on negative connotations of frustration and lack of fulfillment.[32] Concern over excess women reached such a pitch that a proposal was made to ship unmarried women to the colonies, where they might fulfill their "appropriate function" as wives and mothers; such a project had also been proposed by Victorians, a fact that links Victorian and interwar domestic ideology.[33] But in many ways the "modern" attack against the unmarried woman was more virulent, since she was stripped of her Victorian associations with social service and positive contribution.

Smith was to respond to this absurd, although frightening, imagery by variously remixing cultural representations. Sometimes she preserves traditional cultural representations of women, but the images end up in the "wrong" places, with the "wrong" narratives. A mother with children sits underneath a poem concerning a rebellious unmarried woman, for example. A variant of this practice involved reconfiguring cultural imagery. Some of Smith's unhappy love poems are accompanied by a woman with colonial ornamentation: the colonies become an imaginary marginal place or space where a woman might go to escape rather than to achieve a proper domestic role. Smith's poems and drawings thus respond to the romantic colonial fiction of the interwar period by picking up its notions of escapism, yet rejecting its push toward depicting romantic relationships.[34] Smith also mixed contemporary images with those of past discourses such as folklore and fairy tales: Witches and fairies appear as frequent subjects and images in her poetry.

But Smith's combination of visual and verbal constructs is hardly random. Frequently, patterns of juxtaposition are repeated. Smith's specific technique for combining these cultural images is to use the traditional attributes of one art form, visual art, against those of the other, the lyric. As W. J. T. Mitchell points out in *Iconology* (1986), the image has traditionally been considered the word's binary opposite.[35] From Lessing's *Laocoon*, we have inherited a tradition that associates art with space and literature with time.[36] Such oppositions, as Hélène Cixous argues in "Sorties," frequently break down into gender oppositions as well.[37] Mitchell maps Lessing's discourse onto the following chart:

Painting	Poetry
Space	Time
Natural Signs	Arbitrary (man-made) signs
Narrow sphere	Infinite range
Imitation	Expression
Body	Mind
External	Internal
Silent	Eloquent
Beauty	Sublimity
Eye	Ear
Feminine	Masculine[38]

Despite the rigid binarism of such a model, the linearity of the lyric—in Smith's case, narrative lyrics—would seem to enable the rebellious woman creator to break free from the static confines of visual representation.

But for a woman writer, linear time has its own gendered codes, its own binary oppositions. As Rachel DuPlessis outlines, masculine time has been identified with the quest plot, feminine time with the romance.[39] For the woman writer to fulfill her cultural obligations, she must move her female characters to one of two endings, either the euphoric, where the female is incorporated in society through marriage, or the dysphoric, where the rebellious female is expelled from society through death.[40] Linearity and the progress of time, by themselves, are no more freeing to the woman artist than is the static domain of visual art.

Smith's narrative poems and drawings manage to get around the restrictions of binary choices—stasis or movement toward culturally prescribed endings—by mixing the two art forms together. The stasis of visual image is a particularly handy weapon against linear movement that leads to the altar. Linear movement, however, becomes an equally useful weapon against the static iconicity of femininity. Through a mixing of competing traditions, as well as a mixing of discourses and images, Smith was able to halt the culturally repressive images of her day, and at the same time jumpstart the culture with other, less limiting images and stories.

Much of Smith's composite art works against the euphoric ending in an attempt to reveal that romance and marriage were not nearly as "happy" an ending for women as was portrayed in her time. She frequently capitalizes upon the stasis of visual art in order to show the ways in which her culture attempted to trap women through imagery. Narratives that tell tales of rebellious women are often juxtaposed with a drawing that serves to reinforce socially acceptable conventions. Thus, Smith's use of visual art can reveal the way in which the seamless image of woman halts deviant narratives.

But the traditional static quality of art possesses its own subversive effects. It can halt the linearity of those narratives that entice women into concentrating solely on love and romance. Although euphoric endings occur infrequently in Smith's poetry, she will often juxtapose them with an unsettling drawing, one that serves to question the supposed euphoria of the speaker. In more complex pieces, poem and drawing work in conjunction to halt the cultural notion of the euphoric ending.

Far more common in Smith's work, though, is the challenge to the dysphoric ending, which foresees only unhappiness, if not death, for the unmarried woman. As mentioned above, this ending took on particular relevance in the postwar era when being an unmarried woman was so emotionally charged an issue. After all, Smith herself was one of these supposedly miserable spinsters. The dysphoric narrative poem, which surfaces frequently in Smith's writing, is often juxtaposed with a jolly or silly drawing, one that functions to question the supposed exile/death of the unmarried woman. Barbera and McBrien notice the frequency of this pattern, if not its association with women, when they write: "Often, next to poems about rejection, loss and despair, Stevie's childlike drawings playfully wink at the reader. . . ."[41] Smith's poems and drawings thus function together to create new spaces or places for women. In depicting

Figure 3.1. "All Things Pass"

single women as adventurers and creators rather than as withered spinsters, she dealt a blow to the patriarchal society of her time, which increasingly identified women with domesticity.

RESISTING THE EUPHORIC:
IMAGE AS CULTURAL OBSTRUCTION

One of the functions of Smith's poems and drawings is to reveal to the reader/viewer how mass culture's static views of womanhood often work to stop those who challenge romantic and domestic ideologies. Smith's most rebellious poems often seem hemmed in by a conventional drawing placed squarely underneath, or in some cases above, a poem. The escapist nature of her poetic narratives is literally blocked by the image, connecting to the poem almost without white space. Compared with many of Smith's poems and drawings, extravagant in their use of white space, these feel cramped and constricted. Even if a woman writer can veer away from her cultural inheritance of love and romance, these poems and drawings seem to suggest that rebellious narratives can easily dissipate into the culture, given the dominance of domestic ideology.

Smith's cynical love poems sometimes begin or end with a drawing of an ideal home, supposedly woman's greatest prize next to husband and children. Her small poems are literally dwarfed by the overwhelming largeness of the accompanying domestic image. One of the simplest and earliest of these poems is "All Things Pass" (fig. 3.1), originally from *A*

Good Time Was Had by All (1937), though its importance to Smith is sig-
naled by the fact that she chose it as the end poem for her 1966 collection, *The Frog Prince and Other Poems.* The lyric of the poem is unusu-
ally short and straightforward: "All things pass / Love and mankind is
grass."[42] By itself, the poem questions the permanency and stability of
love, one of the foundations of domestic ideology, by pointing out love's
ephemeral nature, so easily ended by either death or the fickleness of
human beings. The poem would seem to be a despairing one, but if read
in the light of Whitman, whom Smith knew early in her career, the poem
becomes more playful.[43] If grass is, as in Whitman's *Leaves of Grass,* a
property of renewal, love and mankind are recyclable as well as expend-
able. Although stable, monogamous love may not last, love itself may be
rekindled or reawakened.

But the poem, which refers to love and humans as organic, natural elements, albeit via Whitman's poetry, is juxtaposed with an extremely non-
natural domestic setting, where a young couple lies kissing on a couch.
Though the couple are the focal point of the drawing, it is their environ-
ment that is noteworthy. Given Smith's typical lack of setting in her drawings, the couple's surroundings—frilly curtains, striped and flowered
wallpaper, a comfortable divan—are amazingly solid and representational. Obviously, the poem, which stresses the impermanence of love, and
the drawing, which underscores the solid, domestic trappings of married
love, are at odds with each other. But what, exactly, this apparent lack of
coherence means is left up to the reader/viewer. Is Smith suggesting that
the solidity of the couple's surroundings is illusory, given the ephemeral
nature of love? Is the poem, therefore, a warning to young girls who bet
their economic futures on the chanciness of romance? Or is the poem a
comment on the relative absence of voices critical to domestic ideology?
After all, the couple appears blissfully unaware of any dangers, and the
cautionary poem is tiny next to the large drawing. Whatever the reader/
viewer's final interpretation, the poem sets up a dialogue between a dissenting voice and a patriarchal culture, one in which the dissenting voice
is visually overwhelmed by the culture.

A poem that reveals more sinister aspects of heterosexual love than its
fickleness is "The Murderer" (fig. 3.2; originally from *Tender Only to
One,* 1938), which like many of Smith's poems deals with domestic violence, most often that of husbands or fathers. In this poem, we hear from
a woman's murderer, presumably her lover or husband. He blames his
love's "diffiden[ce]" for her "accident," apparently her death by his
hand.[44] As Christopher Ricks points out, the awkwardness of the rhyme
"diffident" and "accident" serves only to underscore the link between
the two words.[45] Through the awkward rhyme, Smith mocks the equally

Figure 3.2. "The Murderer"

awkward, and illogical, notion that the woman's reserve, her "crime," merits her death.

Yet the drawing that accompanies the poem reveals nothing of this terrifying violence. As in "All Things Pass," we see a stable domestic setting: frilly curtains, a fireplace with a clock and vases, a carpet, a divan, and even a pet parrot. The couple are in a similar, presumably romantic embrace. But whereas "All Things Pass" is at least partially comical, this poem is chilling, given our lack of knowledge about the time connection between poem and drawing. The girl on the divan might be dead, since her eyes are closed and her mouth is open, but then so are her male lover's eyes closed. If this is a picture of the couple before the "accident," then it would suggest the lie of domesticity, the turbulence and anger that can exist beneath the seemingly tranquil surface. However, even more horrifying is the possibility that the girl is dead, in which case the boyfriend holds his dead lover in a romantic embrace. Does he prefer a dead and therefore even more diffident girl to her live counterpart? Is Smith suggesting that the best woman, for some men anyway, is necessarily a dead one?

In addition to her unconventional love poems, Smith often writes similarly unconventional poems about those who choose to live alone. Richly imaginative, these poems defy the simplistic and restrictive images of

Figure 3.3. "The Heavenly City"

womanhood affixed next to them. "The Heavenly City" (fig. 3.3), originally from *Mother, What Is Man?* (1942), joins an escapist poem with a
crude drawing of a woman, a pairing that eventually reveals both the false
simplicity of societal imagery and its ability to constrain and confine. The
poem opens with its speaker indulging in a vivid fantasy of another world:

> I sigh for the heavenly country,
> Where the heavenly people pass,
> And the sea is as quiet as a mirror
> Of beautiful beautiful glass.
>
> I walk in the heavenly field,
> With lilies and poppies bright,
> I am dressed in a heavenly coat
> Of polished white.[46]

The fantasy grows more and more otherworldly until it ends with its angelic speaker, apparently free from gender, "fly[ing] over the housetops"
and "stand[ing] on the bright moony beams." Such an exquisitely beautiful poem would seem to require an equally lovely drawing, but what we
get instead is a crude, almost ugly drawing of a woman sitting at a table in
a small room. Of course, we cannot positively determine the woman's
marital state, but a number of clues in the drawing suggest that the woman
is unmarried: She sits at a tiny table with only one chair, her apartment
appears too small for another person, and she has the wizened, lonely
look of spinsters in popular culture. By themselves, poem and drawing
are clearly representative, but together they form a puzzle, one that
prompts a reader/viewer to consider the possibilities of connection.

One of the first possibilities is that the speaker in the poem and the woman in the drawing are one and the same, or at least the poem represents that woman transmuted into a genderless being in the other world. Given this reading, the poem serves as a commentary on the restrictiveness of society's simplistic imagery. Hardly the song of a withered spinster, the poem reveals an active and sensuous imagination. Using nature as the traditional escape route from culture, this woman, perhaps prompted by the image of the plant in front of her, flees into a landscape of lilies, poppies, grass, and streams. But as with so many of Smith's women characters, such as Pompey who disappears into the Utrillo painting, the girl who runs away in "The Lady of the Well-Spring," and the typist sucked into the Turner painting in "Deeply Morbid," nature is mediated through culture. Here, though, the poem's cultural referent is verbal rather than visual. The speaker's "heavenly country" recalls Dickinson's poetry in general, as the speaker sees white lilies and wears a "heavenly coat / Of polished white." But more specifically, the poem is analogous to Dickinson's "I Went to Heaven," with its stillness and heavenly people. Both poems are not only nature landscapes, but landscapes of death, another traditional metaphor of escape for literary women. Accepting death as the sentence for rebellious women, both authors reenvision death, using the Christian image of heaven against itself, or, in the Smith poem, combining Christian imagery with that of witchcraft, since one who flies over housetops might be witch rather than angel.

Other possibilities center on a disjunction between the speaker and the drawing, suggesting a contrast between the vivid life of the speaker-dreamer and the lonely, bored spinster. As Judy Little affirms in her study of Muriel Spark, our lives are often channeled through society's pathways: The woman in the drawing seems to have accepted her fate and "become" a spinster.[47] The huge plant on the table mocks the woman, its vitality a contrast with her lack, its phallic shape perhaps a comment on her unfilled sexuality. Accompanied by no friends or lovers, this woman with her plant "becomes" a spinster, apparently unable to repair her discontent. Neither reading of the poem is finally more valid than the other, since both function together to reveal the ways in which culture can free or trap.

The narrative poem entitled "Deeply Morbid" (fig. 3.4), originally from *Harold's Leap* (1950), similarly counters the cultural myth of the lonely, unhappy spinster with the tale of an unmarried female typist who escapes her cares by disappearing into a Turner painting:

> She stood up straight
> The sun fell down
> There was no more of London Town

She went upon the painted shore
And there she walks for ever more
Happy quite
Beaming bright
In a happy happy light
All alone.[48]

She is said to be happy "all alone," despite the fact that her office mates, who continually remark upon her lonely state, feel that solitude is unhealthy, even morbid. They would call the young Featherstonehaugh, perhaps her fiancé, to rescue her, to persuade her to take up a more socially acceptable ending than living in a Turner painting. A contrast to the bored, unmarried typist of *The Waste Land,* Smith's character serves to poke fun at societal pressure by revealing that to be "all alone" is hardly a desperate state, and may be an immensely creative one. The typist's life is championed by the "I" of the poem, who shows up at the end, further endorsing the typist's choice to escape.

But the poem is immediately counteracted with the drawing that follows. Instead of a single typist, we are shown a mother of two, pushing her children in a pram while she shops. The mother is staring off into space, not looking at the children, or the shops. Is Smith's message that individual daydreams are usually coopted by socially mandated dreams, unmarried life leading in sequence to married life? Or is the woman of the drawing the "I" we met at poem's end, envious over the typist's escape? Either way, the drawing shows us a much more mundane world than Joan's: Marriage and motherhood can hardly rival Turner's painted shores.

Smith's poem thus questions the "naturalness" of the romance plot's consequences, the birth of children. The woman in the drawing would seem to have procured woman's "natural" ending through the birth of her children. Yet she is engulfed in society, all but disappearing into the buildings that surround her. It is the typist, instead, who gains the natural world. She, not her married counterpart, gets to sit on nature's shore. Here Smith would seem to be simply inverting the two roles, and thereby suggesting that the single state is actually woman's more natural state. But this reading oversimplifies Smith's composite artwork. The typist disappears not into "real" nature but, as in the previous poem, into a cultural representation of nature, Turner's painting. For Smith, there is no natural world of escape, only that which can be created by a revision of culture. The escape that the poem effects, therefore, is the rethinking of naturalness in our culture and the questioning of all myths of naturalness.

In all four of the above poems, as in others such as "Progression," "Silence and Tears," "The Repentance of Lady T," and "V.," the rebellion of

Figure 3.4. "Deeply Morbid"

the poetry is undercut by the conventionality of the drawing, a juxtaposition that reveals the power of domestic imagery. The poems, so often end-stopped by their drawings, would seem to suggest that escape is impossible. And yet the poems and drawings work together to show that imaginative escape is possible, since Smith brings in other forms of culture: Whitman, Dickinson, and Turner all offer "windows of escape," through death, through nature, through art. Not that these are actual escapes, but they offer a cultural heritage of mechanisms for opposing the dominant culture. As Smith was to write in "My Muse" (1960), republished in *Me Again,* "Poetry is a strong way out."[49]

RESISTING THE EUPHORIC: IMAGE AS NARRATIVE BLOCKER

Very few of Smith's poems feature the euphoric ending of successful romance, but those that do are often undercut by an accompanying drawing. In this case, the static nature of the image stops or prevents the linearity of the traditional romance. For Smith, romance always contains a menacing aspect, never to be forgotten in the happiness of the moment. Interestingly, these poems of successful romance occur *before* marriage, either directly after the speaker falls in love or when the speaker is only contemplating marriage. No female speaker ever exhibits a euphoric ending in a married state. As one of Smith's characters says, "Though a marriage be fairly sprung / And the heart be loving and giving, / In the end it is sure to go wrong."[50]

Often Smith's drawings require us to rethink apparent love poems. For example, Smith's "Conviction (iv)" (fig. 3.5), originally from *Mother, What Is Man?* (1942), seems to be a poem that celebrates the joys of love, both sexual and emotional, as it declares that "[t]here is no bliss like

63

Figure 3.5. "Conviction (iv)"

this."[51] Love is held to be an extremely safe, secure state, since the speaker declares, "I like to be held and tightly kissed, / Safe from all alarms." Heterosexual romance would appear to be a safe haven, opposed to the potentially violent and dangerous world outside its sheltering ring. We do not know whether the speaker of the poem is male or female, but the speaker's equation of love with safety and emotional satisfaction suggests that the speaker is a woman, these traits being the ones women associate with traditional marriage. On first reading, then, Smith's poem largely underscores rather than challenges the conventional promises of love, despite its punning on "get off" in the first line.

However, the drawing accompanying the poem is highly unsettling and threatens to undermine the bliss presented in the poem. Barbera and McBrien suggest that the figure of the animal is the puzzling center of the composite text, since it may represent a watchdog in a park or a lion in a jungle.[52] Whether dog or lion, the figure adds an element of menace and reminds us of the isolated state of the young woman, far away from any social intervention. Whether the female of the drawing is currently happy or not, the isolation of the romantic state is revealed as potentially precarious rather than certainly safe. Such a representation of romance's dangers is hardly unique to this poem, since other Smith poems tell of men's violence, or potential violence, in faraway forests, as in "Who Shot Eugenie." Elsewhere the colonial "other" of the forest (complete with lion) is used in Smith's work as a place of escape, but she can also draw, as in the above poem, on the more traditional connections between the colonial "other" and fearful, dark desires. The drawing then leads us to reconsider the poem, for, as Barbera and McBrien have pointed out "There is no bliss like this" can mean "such bliss is beyond compare" or "such bliss does not exist (except in imagination)."[53]

Figure 3.6. "The Hat"

Another poem that questions the happy bliss of the euphoric ending is "The Hat" (fig. 3.6), originally from *Harold's Leap* (1950); like "Conviction (iv)," it presents the potential dysphoria of even the most happy of endings, a point made clear by Smith in her "Poems and Drawings III" introduction: "[M]arriage is not always a solution of problems, though this girl, fancy-fed in a dream of rich hats, seems to think it is."[54] The young girl in the poem dreams of a marriage in which her identity, represented by her delight in her hat, will coexist with the romantic union between her and her future husband. The girl never questions the incompatibility of individual desires with romantic union, but asserts: "The King will marry me and make me his own before all / And when I am married I shall wear my hat and walk on the palace wall."[55] Presumably, she thinks that she can be the King's "own" and yet do whatever she pleases, i.e., "walk on the palace wall."

However, the woman's face in the drawing accompanying the poem raises questions. Her expression could be read as tensely fearful, perhaps because she is about to lose the hat she clutches with both hands. Hats in Smith's poems often represent women's freedom, as in "My Hat." Smith

65

Figure 3.7. "Mrs. Simpkins"

herself once noted that "There are a great many hats in my poems. They represent going away and also running away."[56] But the girl's ability to preserve her freedom is in question here. Does her holding of her hat suggest that she is destined to mature into a young woman who must continually guard against the loss of her identity? Or does her solitude suggest that she will choose possession of her hat, and perhaps loneliness, over the company of king and husband? Additionally, her expression could be read as obsessively dreamy. Marriage is clearly a material exchange for the girl—hat for ring—and involves a threat of loss: "The King will . . . make me his own." In this light, walking on the palace wall becomes a more sinister and less playful act.

In the above examples, the drawings undermine or undercut the overly sweet optimism of the poetry, yet poem and drawing may also work in complex relation with each other by requiring the reader/viewer's attention to go back and forth multiple times between text and illustration. An example of such complex representation is the early "Mrs. Simpkins" (fig. 3.7), originally from *A Good Time Was Had by All* (1937). The poem begins by narrating the fairly ordinary life of a Mrs. Simpkins, a middle-class married woman who "never ha[s] very much to do."[57] Able to amuse herself as she wishes, she spends her time pondering the truth of the Trinity, which she has begun to doubt. Thus far, Smith's portrait of Mrs. Simpkins is largely descriptive: she is an unremarkable person of a particular class and time.

However, only four lines into the poem, the poem is disrupted by the drawing of an older, wrinkled woman, surprisingly dressed as a 1920s flapper, complete with dropped waist and short skirt. The drawing would seem to be connected to the poem's previous line: "And that things had moved very far since the days of her youth." At first, the drawing merely suggests, like the poem, that Mrs. Simpkins' beliefs are outdated. Yet the flapper costume also insinuates a connection between Mrs. Simpkins and the culture that produced her. Is her silliness at least partially the result of a culture that assigned the role of pleasure seeking and romance to the young women of her day?

The rest of the poem, like the drawing, questions the culture's education of women, particularly in married life, as Mrs. Simpkins is left impoverished because she fails to understand the ways in which she is dependent upon her husband. Having been told by Mrs. Simpkins that eternal life will keep them together forever, her husband shoots himself to escape her at least temporarily, leaving Mrs. Simpkins to "polish the floors of Westminster County Hall for her daily bread." Though Mrs. Simpkins is foolish, Mark Storey rightly claims that she has gotten "a raw deal," since she has not been in a position to understand hard economic realities.[58] The flat affect of the poem's last line holds out little sympathy to Mrs. Simpkins, yet the drawing of the aging flapper that is associated with Mrs. Simpkins is pitiable.

A later example of poem and drawing working together to stop the romance plot is "The Wedding Photograph" (fig. 3.8), originally from *Selected Poems* (1962). In this poem, Smith conflates the euphoric and dysphoric endings of the romance plot, thereby undermining the culture's distinction between a woman's success and failure. The poem presents a young woman's thoughts as she is posing for her wedding photographs, and would therefore seem to be a perfect example of a romance with a happy ending. However, the poem, by starting with a wedding, reverses or inverts the typical line of the romance plot. Besides, this wedding is hardly a happy occasion: the speaker has merely married Harry, her husband, in order to get away from her home.

In addition, the poem also contains something of the dysphoric romance. The union between Harry and the speaker is scheduled to end in death, although such an ending has not yet occurred. The speaker's meditation on her husband Harry's death suggests that she will be party to his

Figure 3.8. "The Wedding Photograph"

demise, since she looks forward to her husband's being devoured by a lion on their honeymoon trip, leaving her "alone on the jungle path."[59] This poem, then, reverses Smith's usual pattern of women's death in the jungle. How the woman is going to get the lion to cooperate with her is unclear, but in this poem nature is woman's ally in securing freedom from her married state. The colonial forest becomes woman's friend, not because of her ability to locate a mate in the colonies, as in contemporary lore, but because of her ability to *dispose* of a mate in the dark jungle. As in "Conviction (iv)," Smith sometimes reverts to an older, darker reading of the jungle, although here that darker reading is more positive.

It is important to note, however, that the poem is not simply an inversion of euphoric and dysphoric stories conjoined together, since Harry's death has not yet taken place. Will his new bride eventually be free of him? How will she create the conditions for his death? Her curse at the end of the poem can be read as either a curse of despair or else a witch's attempt to influence the future: "Ah woe, burn fire, burn in eyes' sheathing / Fan bright fear, fan fire in Harry's breathing." Thus, we as readers are left unable to decide where the poem is going.

The relationship between the text and the drawing is even more problematic than in the previous poems. The illustration of a poem on the wedding photograph should, it seems, present us with the topic of the poem, a portrait of the young couple. But we see no such young couple. Instead, the poem is illustrated with the drawing of a young girl, seemingly dressed for a party. The identity of the girl is perplexing, given her disjunction from the narrative of the poem. Is she the speaker? Indeed, this is the identification that Janice Thaddeus makes in her reading of the poem.[60] Such an identification could lead us to read the bride's narrative as a tragedy, since the young, giggling girl is now a woman married to a man she intends to kill. However, the message is more positive if we read the young girl as a subversive child who continues to be a subversive, although deadly, adult. In this case, marriage does not seem to have dampened the girl's intention to fly in the face of social convention.

Yet another reading, one that disassociates the girl from the bride, is possible. Perhaps the girl is not the speaker at all, but an attendant at the wedding. Indeed, she looks as though she is dressed for a wedding. Is her giggle a sign that young girls are even less seduced by the romance plot than the young, murderous bride? Or does her giggle signify her intent to stay clear of weddings altogether? Her large hat, Smith's emblem of identity and freedom, would seem to be some guarantee of a different life. No reading is certain, but Smith's composite art manages to create an opening in the closed form of the romance plot whereby alternative stories can flourish. One of these is the desperate act of the bride murdering her husband, therefore ending the romance. The other is the defiance of the rebellious girl. Together these stories with their complex ambiguities work to disrupt the formulaic closure mandated for women, as well as their lack of mobility, reinforced by their identification with static images.

The above poems reveal Smith either remixing images from the present, or again, as in the above section, contrasting past and present imagery. In her hands, the present and the familiar become disturbingly unfamiliar. Her flapper is not young and full of life, but old, having reaped no rewards from an early life of pleasure seeking. Her young girls are not innocent, but more mature than the speakers of the poems they accompany. Her colonial forests may be a place of escape, as in contemporary romance novels, though that escape little resembles the novels' emphasis on heterosexual love. Nevertheless, images of the past are never far off in Smith's work. Her use of the forest often refers back to more traditional associations of the forest with darkness and evil: that darkness and evil can be a representation of the patriarchal culture's violence against women, or, because women and forests share associations with darkness, the dark forest can mark woman's revenge against the domesticated world of patriarchy.

Figure 3.9. "Rothebât"

RESISTING THE DYSPHORIC: IMAGES OF ALTERNATIVE SPACES

Far more common in Smith's work is the poem where the dysphoric ending is questioned, as in the four poems below and others such as "Death
of Mr Mounsel," "The Boat," "Siesta," "Bog-Face," and "Venus When
Young Choosing Death." Of course, according to the traditional narrative, the woman who does not succeed in achieving a married state must
be shoved out of society, through death or other forms of marginality. In
fact, many of Smith's poems give voice to the conventional narrative.
However, their accompanying drawings frequently belie such an ending.
Next to mournful love poems, Smith frequently places self-contented,
even joyous, drawings of women.

An early example is "Rothebât" (fig. 3.9), originally from *Tender
Only to One* (1938). The poem itself is extremely mournful, as the female
speaker presents her pain at the loss of her love, Rothebât. The speaker
masochistically takes on the responsibility for the end of the relationship,
although she does not know what she has done. That the speaker's death
is imminent is revealed by her extremely distraught state. She describes her
heart as "twisted and torn."[61] Such agony and the subsequent self-blame
that the female endures are typical of the dysphoric plot, where the female
is held responsible for the emotional health of the relationship.

Yet the drawing that accompanies this poem tells us nothing of the
speaker's agony; indeed, it seems to be mistakenly paired with its sor-

70

Figure 3.10. "Cool as a Cucumber"

rowful poem. We see a solitary and joyous woman walking off into the page's white space, following what may be a plank into the ocean, or merely a road to nowhere. Here Smith's heroine resembles the figures in Lear's drawings, who often look off into the white space, as if they could see a reality that we cannot.[62] Of course, her exit into blankness may be an exit into death, death being the most typical exit for the dysphoric romantic heroine, but if so, she is hardly perturbed or unhappy. This poem resembles others by Smith, such as "Bog-Face" and "Venus When Young Choosing Death," which figure escape more specifically through a colonial ornamentation that opposes the colonial version of the romance plot.

Perhaps the best example of Smith's resistance toward the dysphoric is "Cool as a Cucumber" (fig. 3.10; *Harold's Leap* [1950]), which features its drawing only in the first edition, not in the *Collected Poems* compiled after Smith's death. The female of the poem, Mary, has grown "nervy grim and bold" and "does not do as she is told."[63] Such disobedience has made her "unfit for marriage" to the miller's son. The speaker, an unidentified voice, closes the poem by saying that Mary will not be seen again, which can mean either that she will die outside the sheltering ring of society, or else, more menacingly, that any woman who does not cooperate will be disposed of.

71

Figure 3.11. "Not Waving but Drowning"

However, in the drawing that accompanies the poem, the girl figured, presumably Mary, is smiling and seemingly happy. She is dressed in a fanciful manner, as if she has joined the fairies—her gloves and tights are striped, what appear to be amulets dangle from her necklace, and a large flower adorns her hair. Here Smith is using the discourse of fairy tales, which have always claimed a cultural "outside" against dominant discourses, here the discourse of romance. In the fairy tale, there is another world made available to the reader, one that encourages us to travel beyond known boundaries. The playful, fairylike Mary of the drawing in no way connects with the distraught, anxious Mary of the poem, which leaves us questioning the social voices we have heard. As Romana Huk points out, Mary is constructed out of the voices we hear; we never actually hear the voice of Mary herself.[64]

The way in which the obviously romance-oriented poems function can perhaps clarify other poems about exile accompanied by cheerful drawings, despite the fact that these poems do not seem to deal with romance. One of these is the famous "Not Waving but Drowning" (fig. 3.11) from the 1957 volume of the same name. The drawing that accompanies this poem in *Collected Poems,* and that reflects the presentation in the original volume *Not Waving but Drowning,* is of a girl with wet hair. We see her from the waist up, seemingly bobbing in the water. Curiously, her hair covers her face, allowing us to see only a mysterious smile. Yet Smith sometimes moved her drawings to other poems, which is the case with this girl, since the drawing shows up as the illustration of another poem, "The Frozen Lake," in *Selected Poems.*[65]

The initial poem, "Not Waving but Drowning," would not seem to have anything to do with femininity, since the poem treats a male speaker who is drowning or has drowned:

> Nobody heard him, the dead man,
> But still he lay moaning:
> I was much further out than you thought
> And not waving but drowning.[66]

But as Janice Thaddeus points out, there is an odd juxtaposition between the gender of the speaker and that of the figure in the drawing.[67] After all, why place a picture of a seemingly satisfied girl next to a poem of a drowning man? The contrast could suggest that a man who ventures outside society's boundaries drowns, but a female survives and even flourishes. The poem indirectly comments on the romance plot, since to be "outside" brings life, not death, for women.

Smith moved this image of the bobbing girl to "The Frozen Lake" in *Selected Poems* (1962), an iconic tie that provides an even stronger connection for two poems that are already thematically connected: They both tell stories of those who wander beyond the limits. But whereas "Not Waving but Drowning" is about general transgression, "The Frozen Lake" is about a specific one, writing poetry.

The poem opens with the speaker taking on the masculine quest plot, to find the lady of the lake. Already there is transgression, since Smith, after all, is the female author who presents herself as a quester. The poem, by itself, would seem to suggest that such a transgression is doomed to failure; in a world structured by gender opposition, one cannot unite the masculine persona with the feminine self. The quester/poet is impaled upon the phallic sword, and [his] blood dyes the water:

> And so I died, and the lake-water
> That holds the form of Ullan's daughter
> With all my blood is dyed,
> Is dyed,
> With all my love is dyed.[68]

Blood replaces ink; the only sign of [his] existence is body rather than art. The woman poet's attempt to act as quester would seem to be vanquished by the specificity of her gender, her blood dissipating into nothingness in the water.

However, the presence of the drawing, on the margins of the text, indicates another possibility. After all, the poem is finished, and Lord Ullan's daughter, the witch, apparently survives. Perhaps the drawing of the woman outsider means that women authors need not take up the male identity of quester any more than they need take up their traditional identity as wives and mothers. Through "outside" images—in this case, the witch—the role of the woman writer can be transformed. The quester's breaking of the ice and subsequent death split open the witch's kingdom to the outside world. No longer need she be condemned to tapping on ice.

While Smith's composite art can glance back to the freeing images of the romantics, or play with the images of her culture, she can also search the more distant past for imagery to pit against the dominant discourse of domestic ideology. Some of Smith's favorite discourses in the grab bag of the past were fairy tales and folklore, a traditional repertory of rebellious women. Smith, who herself was often thought of as a witch by the children in her neighborhood, used the discourses of childhood against that of the adult world, not, as some have suggested, to glorify the world of the child, but to undermine the very distinction between the free child and the bound adult. Smith's art questions whether the bound adult, so often a woman, really need remain bound, given that other discourses exist that might free her.

For many years, Smith's poems, if they have been read at all, have been read without their drawings. Without these, Smith's poems do still survive as critiques of romance, but much of their combative force is lost. We miss the split-screen effect of her art, which remixes imagery of her time period, many times combining it with images of the past. Such a use of the past is not nostalgic, as it often is in works by male modernists such as T. S. Eliot and Ezra Pound, but looks forward to a world beyond gendered hierarchies. Some might read Smith's work as merely destructive, one that pulls apart the fabric of the culture, but like Mary Kelly's, it also reconstructs. Griselda Pollock's description of Mary Kelly's art might easily be applied to Smith:

It implies an advance upon the disciplines and deconstructions . . . which Laura Mulvey has labelled "negative aesthetics," remodelled to deal with new materials at a new moment. Visually cued humour and wit acknowledge but interrupt the evident pleasure which feminists now recognize as securing complicity with the images of femininity. In place of the abstract spectator of earlier theorizations, the work addresses a social spectator . . . who is invited to share a learning process which moves across the images and tropes of the dominant culture. . . .[69]

The humor and wild play of Smith's art cause us to laugh at traditional depictions of femininity and to note that the windows of escape have always existed. As Regina Barreca asserts, "Women's humour is about our reclamation of certain forms of control over our own lives."[70] Through Smith's cultural irreverence, the reader/viewer is encouraged to participate in discourses that counter traditional representations of femininity, thereby undermining its dominance. Smith's art sets off a chain reaction that, to use Irigaray's words, "rack[s] (the culture) . . . with radical convulsions."[71]

4

The Book Reviews

1941–1951

In their 1979 essay "[Why] Are There No Great Women Critics?" Susan Sniader Lanser and Evelyn Torton Beck applaud the efforts of feminist scholars to recover and study women's literature, but point out that "no similar body of material has been uncovered" for women critics.[1] Citing literature's connection to such traditionally feminine traits as "sensitivity, expressiveness, and sensuality," and criticism's linkage to such masculine traits as "logic, judgment, and the ability to abstract," they claim that the literary world still reflects the binary divisions of the traditional gender construct.[2] Although their essay is now over fifteen years old, their statement is still largely valid, and even more disturbing, given the amount of time that has passed. Although no longer "rarely anthologized," Virginia Woolf is still the only twentieth-century British woman writer to have achieved status as an important critic.[3] Lanser and Beck rightly suggest that feminist scholars should turn at least some of their recovery efforts toward women critics, many of whom crossed genres in writing both literature and criticism.[4] As one of London's most entertaining and well-known book reviewers, Stevie Smith is a critical voice that has been ignored too long.

Smith reviewed in over sixteen contemporary periodicals, some of them for periods of ten or fifteen years.[5] These periodicals vary from popular Newnes publications, such as *John O'London's Weekly,* which Smith herself once called a "tripey rag,"[6] to well-respected publications such as the *Spectator,* the *New Statesman,* the *Observer,* and the *Listener.* Her range of reviewing topics was similarly varied: she covered novels, nonfiction, some poetry, religious works, social and political treatises, and an occasional art publication. Her reviews focus largely on the work at hand, but they also often contain statements on readers and reading, critics and reviewing, aesthetics and politics, and literature and the literary. Why then has Smith's critical record been ignored?

Many factors appear to have contributed. One of these, no doubt, is Smith's reputation as literary outsider. The myth of the marginalized Stevie of Palmer's Green has prevented an acknowledgment of her as a London reviewer, with the literary connections that role necessarily entails. Another factor is that Smith largely reviewed fiction and nonfiction, choices not in keeping with her more established role as famous poet. In fact, she often declined to review poetry. Then there is her lack of respect for the hierarchical divisions of the literary world: She reviewed for the "tripey rags" as well as for "high" art publications.

And finally, there is the question of her enjoyment of literary reviewing and her subsequent investment in it as a genre. As Barbera and McBrien point out, Smith's interest in reviewing was largely financial.[7] However, in quoting one of Smith's letters, they also note that she was not paid for some of her early reviewing stints.[8] At least initially, Smith was motivated by reasons other than financial ones, most likely the desire to keep her name and the name of women writer friends in the limelight. Certainly, Smith reviewed a staggering number of books and often felt that her reviewing was interfering with her poetry, but Smith's reviews themselves never manifest exhaustion, nor a lack of interest in the reviewing process. Frances Spalding attests that Smith was a trusted professional.[9]

Those few critics attending to Smith's reviews have done so briefly, often imposing a simple linear pattern on her career. For example, Spalding suggests that Smith used her experience with Newnes publications to eventually work her way "up" or "onward" to the more prestigious literary journals: "Such work fed her knowledge of contemporary fiction and left her very well practised, able, at a later date to emerge as a distinctive, authoritative voice in the pages of the *Spectator,* the *New Statesmen,* the *Observer,* and the *Listener.*"[10] Certainly, Smith's early reviews were briefer and covered less-well-remembered works, but Spalding's characterization of these early reviews as apprentice work largely discounts one of Smith's most interesting reviewing stints, especially for feminist scholars: her ten years of writing for *Modern Woman,* published by her employer, Newnes. Hardly a "high" art publication, *Modern Woman* was one of those women's magazines that Smith had deplored in *Novel on Yellow Paper.*

Started in the interwar period, *Modern Woman,* like others, continued Victorian domestic ideology by concentrating on home and family. As opposed to *Woman,* the period's most popular women's magazine, *Modern Woman* possessed a small percentage of the total readership (though it

shared this low level of readership with a number of other magazines).
In the 1939 IIPA survey, 1.53 percent of the women surveyed had read
Modern Woman, compared with the 10.23 percent who regularly read
Woman. Though *Modern Woman* was more conservative in its presentation of gender roles, the two magazines' readerships were similar; both
catered largely to middle-class women between the ages of twenty-five
and forty-four.[11] As did many such magazines, it addressed the "new"
housewife who needed training in the pragmatics of domesticity. According to Martin Pugh,

If there is any change at all after 1918 it is in the form of a shift of emphasis away
from the somewhat fuzzy, idealised view of married life towards a more practical
approach. This is reflected in the titles of the many new papers that sprang up in
the 1920's—*Woman and Home, My Home, Modern Woman, Modern Home, Wife
and Home.*[12]

How and why Smith participated in such a media form are crucial to
an account of her as a feminist and opponent of domestic ideology, as well
as a creative and groundbreaking reviewer. Unfortunately, the Pearson-
Newnes correspondence between Smith and her editors has been lost, but
the reviews themselves survive. Anyone who flips through old issues of
Modern Woman, reading first the contents of the magazine and then
Smith's reviews, will be immediately aware of the dissonance created by
the content and style of her reviews. While the magazine maintains a
chirrupy and sometimes syrupy tone, Smith's reviews are playful, ironic,
and, at times, even savage. Whatever her intention, her reviews seriously
disrupt the conservative gender ideology of the magazine.

Smith's radical disruptions occur through her challenge to the traditional, hierarchical relationship between reviewer and reader. In this way,
Smith differentiated herself from other modernists who maintained a distinction between "high" and "low" reviewing, as well as between "high" and
"low" art. Although Virginia Woolf was to set herself up as one "common
reader" speaking to another, her maintenance of the distinction between
professional critic and general reader shows her unable or unwilling to let
go of traditional hierarchies.[13] Smith makes no such distinction: She re-
sponds to her audience as a diverse group of readers, neither elite nor common. Additionally, Smith was to encourage her women readers to think for
themselves and make their own choices of reading material, unlike Woolf
who did not enter women's mass culture market. Thus, Smith's reviews
in *Modern Woman* attempt to shake women loose from their traditional
role as passive readers and consumers, teaching them instead to break the
binary division between masculine producers and feminine receivers.

Such an interpretation of Smith's reviews in *Modern Woman* involves reading her career backward, since some of her most radical reviewing occurs earlier, for understandable reasons having to do with the gendered divisions of the literary world. Smith's reviews in more prestigious literary publications provide crucial records of her beliefs and views, yet they largely conform to the conventions of elite literary reviewing, and thus make somewhat less interesting critical and theoretical statements. Of course, for a woman writer to cross over from literature's world of feeling to the critic's world of judgment is, in and of itself, a radical move. But Smith's reviews in the *Spectator* and other such magazines, while sometimes outrageous in their opinions, largely preserve the conventions of the reviewer as expert judge and the reader as willing receiver of the reviewer's expert opinions.

That this form of reviewing is often the preferred and expected type is suggested in Herbert Lindenberger's assessment of reviewing styles. Initially, Lindenberger claims that four forms of reviewing exist:

1. The All-Outer. Notable above all for its totality of response, which manifests itself in an unmitigatingly positive or negative form.

2. The Niggler. Refuses to generalize about the book as a whole or to place it within its appropriate intellectual tradition, but concentrates instead on individual details.

3. The Displacer. Displacement of the author by the reviewer, who ignores the book supposedly under review to concentrate on his own concerns.

4. The Summarizer. Restates some of the book's main points, often by citation of chapter titles and whatever generalizations catch the reviewer's eye.[14]

Yet Lindenberger, as does a later commentator on his work, reveals his preference for judgment:

Yet nearly all reviews . . . commit themselves to either a predominantly positive or negative stance; however much the reviewer may qualify his statements, a glance down the page of most reviews shows a preponderance of strong epithets conventionally used either for praise or condemnation.[15]

Lindenberger's statements suggest that the preferred stance of the literary reviewer is still the role of paternalistic judge.

Smith was to advocate and defend the traditional reviewer's role in "Statement on Criticism" (1958), originally published in the *P.E.N. News*, now available in *Me Again*. Here Smith herself uses the judicial metaphor:

A critic is meant to be a judge. So he must have the judging qualities. What are these? First—attention. . . . Then he must be impartial.[16]

The essay is most radical in its recognition that reviewers have not always been impartial in their judgment:

"There are too many women novelists," I heard a critic say (a very much indulged and important one, too). Turn it the other way: "There are too many men novelists," and how absurd it is.[17]

But this comment, despite its sympathy for women novelists, does not question the hierarchical role of the reviewer, which has often functioned, and still continues to function, as a means of silencing women's voices, as both writers and readers.

And yet Smith's adoption of this traditionally masculine role did to a certain extent disrupt the literary hierarchy. By maintaining an elitist role in prestige magazines, Smith was to further her career and that of other women writers. After all, she was a *woman* adopting the persona of judge. Through mimicry of the traditional reviewer's voice, Smith was to assert herself into the literary hierarchy, thus keeping her name current. In addition, Smith was frequently a sympathetic judge of other women writers. Sometimes hurt by the reviews of others, particularly those of women friends such as Inez Holden and Rosamond Lehmann, Smith was a generous reviewer who almost never completely dismissed a book. Although she wrote a mixed review for Olivia Manning's *The Doves of Venus,* Smith was largely an advocate of Manning's work, as well as that of others. She actively pushed the works of Inez Holden and Kay Dick, through both reviewing and attempting to find them publishers.[18] Working within the system enabled Smith to bring women writers from the margins into the fold.

But speaking to an audience of traditional, middle-class women apparently required another voice and a questioning of conventions. Of course, there was already a difference in voice between the literary periodical and the women's magazine. Editors of women's magazines tend to address women readers directly as friends and companions, suggesting a closing of the distance between producer and reader. But of course this technique often masks the very real power relationships that exist between editor and reader. Despite the solicitation of their comments and letters, the female readers of women's magazines are frequently lectured to and literally—through advertisements—sold a bill of goods. The sisterly tone of editorial commentary often masks a dominating matriarchy, its hierarchical attitudes toward its readers as firmly in place as those in the most elite of literary journals.

In *Modern Woman,* Smith was to disrupt this dominating matriarchy, as well as its dissemination of domestic ideology. If the 1958 P.E.N. article acts as her statement on reviewing in more recognizable literary journals, her December 1946 book page, complete with drawing, represents her critical statement on reviewing in *Modern Woman.* As was, and is, common in women's magazines, Smith opens by directly addressing her audience:

Do you make the best use of your Book Page? The best use is to ferret out the books you like and to keep an eye on the author, for what he has written before, and for what he may write again.[19]

Here Smith encourages women to read what interests them by "ferreting it out," i.e., finding what may not be readily available or the first title that comes to mind. Given the conservative gender roles of *Modern Woman,* such advice not only marks support for individual taste but also indicates a recognition of women's limited reading choices. Smith encourages her women readers beyond the familiar boundaries of romantic fiction and domestic advice articles, most of what was published in *Modern Woman.*

Not only does Smith encourage women to read what they like, but she also gives them advice on how to *get* what they like:

A word about public libraries. They will always, if pressed sufficiently hard (you do the pressing) get for you any book that you want, provided that it is a non-fiction book. This means that all history, criticism, biography, poetry, is at your beck and call. Make a nuisance of yourself in pursuit of a good book, it is a good cause.[20]

Her use of "good" book here and later in the review would seem to keep a hierarchy of books in place, but what Smith actually asserts is that any woman may, if she likes, read books from previously unknown categories. Her generalized conclusion on a book by Powys—"It is the Best and it is for you"—is an invitation to invade categories of literature outside the romance, specifically history, criticism, biography, and poetry.[21] The genres Woolf advocates for the woman writer in "Women and Fiction," Smith adopts for the woman reader.[22]

Although a notable voice difference exists between Smith's *Modern Woman* reviews and her reviews in a publication such as the *Spectator,* Smith's reviewing character cannot finally be determined by divisions between the popular and the literary. Her 1958 essay on T. S. Eliot's *Murder in the Cathedral,* a third statement on reviewers and readers, appears in that most elite of literary publications, a birthday tribute to a well-established writer. In this instance, Smith's essay, which she called a most "un-birthday present," is relentlessly harsh on the play, but uses a playful and engaging tone, intended to draw a reader to an understanding of her point of view.[23] Here Smith boldly ignores conventions by refusing Eliot his tribute, instead giving him a rather severe dressing down, as though she is determined to interrupt the act of literary canonization that a birthday tribute implies. Deploring Eliot's social and political hierarchies, Smith advises readers to approach his plays with a "cool" mind, presumably a resistant one.[24] That Smith advocates resistant reading in this situation and in *Modern Woman* suggests that she was able to adapt her reviewing style to her rhetorical situation, using a style that encourages resistant reading when she was most disturbed by the implications of a book. Interestingly, Smith was to use this nonhierarchical reviewing style, one that collapses distance between reviewer and reader, in reviewing situations that were intended to reinforce divisions between readers, in *Modern Woman* between the woman reader of "light" fiction and the more serious reader, and in the Eliot essay between the elite group who recognize Eliot's greatness and the unenlightened who do not. In both, she encourages readers to question the socially produced hierarchies that determine value and access.

MODERN WOMAN GOES TO WAR

Smith's concern about women readers in the 1940s may at first appear unwarranted, given women's roles during the forties, at least during wartime. After all, Smith began reviewing for *Modern Woman* in 1941, a time when British women were supposed to have laid aside domestic roles for those demanded by war: munitions worker (the so-called industrial army), member of the armed forces (as part of the WAAF, WRNS, or ATS), farmer in the Women's Land Army, or participant in the Home Guard, the Women's Voluntary Service, or the Women's Home Defence Organization (the latter learned ju-jitsu and how to throw grenades).[25] Even the period's propaganda often counteracts domestic ideology, a surprising fact since portrayals of women's lives often lag behind the roles they actually perform. However, in many respects domestic ideology continued alive and well during the war. According to Martin Pugh, wartime change did not bring about "an uncomplicated matter of emancipation," and "in some respects it turned out to be distinctly conservative in character."[26]

Although British women were conscripted for war work during World War II, more women stayed at home than participated in the war effort. During the peak of mobilization in 1943, 7,250,000 women were working in industry, the armed forces, and civil defense, but 8,770,000 stayed at home as full-time housewives.[27] Single women were "called up," but married women with children under fourteen and even married women with only their husbands to attend to were given a "Household R" exemption status.[28] Penny Summerfield cites the exasperation that some women felt toward those who were allowed to stay home:

A friend in her twenties went to Labour Exchange on Friday for interviews after registration months ago. "I see you are married. Does your husband come home to his mid-day meal?" "Yes." "Very well, I expect you have enough to do so we won't keep you." The larger lunacy again.[29]

Allowing a woman to stay home for such a relatively minor purpose reveals the British government's fear of tampering with traditional notions, even in the face of labor shortages. Despite the fact that exempt housewives were eventually used in part-time work, war work did little to shake the societal belief that married women belonged at home, even if all they had to do was make lunch.

Not only were the majority of women still home, but most of them were doing even more of the traditional "women's work." Despite the drop in housekeeping standards, women did not have as many goods and services available: women's labor in the home was needed to replace the lack of industrial time spent on consumer goods. Neither did the homemaker's official image change. As Summerfield explains,

Mothers and housewives were shown in domestic settings, wearing high-heels and broad-shouldered coats or frilly pinafores. They were urged to 'Make Do and Mend' . . . the symbol of the economical maintenance of a healthy wartime population, well fed and clothed within the constraints of wartime shortages.[30]

Although the government needed women in the factories, it also needed women's labor in the home, as well as the stabilizing imagery of the traditional homemaker.

It was largely women's magazines that served to domesticate the war (a war already being fought at home) and to cheer up these women who had to make do and mend. As a result, women's magazines during the wartime years were in some ways even more incessantly domestic than in previous years. After all, the writers of women's magazines were the ones teaching British women how to make handknit stockings (to replace silk ones) and marmite rissoles (to substitute for meat dishes). They offered comfort through the most traditional of routes, encouraging women to take pride in their homes, even though those homes might be bombed any day. Suggesting that domestic comfort was simply an impossibility during war or that males (younger and older males were still at home) might make the rissoles seems never to have occurred to editors of these magazines. Summerfield points out the double standard:

Women could be prosecuted for avoiding work in 'men's jobs' for the war effort if they did not come within one of the exemption categories, but men were given no encouragement to take a share of 'women's work' in the home. In spite of the demands of the war effort, the feminine identification of the job of running a home remained undented.[31]

In many ways, then, women were encouraged, as they had been before the war, to concentrate on house and home, as a way of fulfilling both national interests and their own emotional needs.

Modern Woman serves as an example of a magazine that managed to maintain its cheerful and breezy domesticity throughout the darkest years of the war. A review of the contents of *Modern Woman* from February 1941, the first issue in which Smith's book page appeared, easily proves this point.[32] Each of the magazine's departments managed to work the war into women's traditional interests in romance and domesticity, so that domesticity might continue undisturbed. As Martin Pugh attests, morale during the war was at its lowest among married women, those who largely stayed home and coped with wartime shortages.[33] Yet the magazine's editors nevertheless felt that women could be cheered by a continued emphasis on "home."

Although wartime would not seem to offer much in the way of romantic opportunity, to the married woman at home anyway, the stories in the February 1941 issue emphasize that romance and war can coexist. In the serial story "Torpedo," by Patricia Wentworth, the heroine, Beth Langton, meets a new love on the deck of a torpedoed ship. Even though the ship is sinking and they are threatened with death in the ice-cold ocean, Beth and Darrell manage to exchange one last romantic look:

She looked up at him, and for a moment the light was on her face, giving him a picture that he was never to forget—the broad brow with its frame of wind-tossed hair, the shadowed eyes steady on his, the pale lips bent to a lovely, generous smile.[34]

The deck of a sinking ship can be made a temporary home, the story suggests, if one happens to have a couple in love. Another story, told in letters, relates the heroine Pearl's hectic attempt to marry her sailor Neill before he leaves for war; they do marry and he does leave, but with Pearl more delighted by thoughts of "eternal love" than preoccupied with his potential death.[35] According to *Modern Woman*, war is hardly a deterrent to woman's "natural" desires for love and marriage, nor, apparently, to their fulfillment, whether that be a romance on a burning deck or marriage to a departing soldier.

In addition to the traditional romances, the issue provides advice and aid in coping with the war's lack of domestic comforts. According to *Modern Woman*, almost anything can be made by hand, from lingerie to suits. And of course there are recipes, with many of them focusing on ingredients available during wartime. Perhaps the strangest features in the February 1941 issue are those that give instructions on domesticating or making a home out of air raid shelters. Apparently, a woman can, and should, make a home out of whatever structure she finds. There is a tip for making a movable baby's bed out of a laundry basket, suitable for carrying a child into a shelter and keeping him warm throughout the night.[36] Another article focusing on shelter comfort is Mary Gilbert's Home News Page, which carries an ad for a comfortable and lightweight stool on which to sit in a crowded shelter. Even a shelter, according to Gilbert, needs its furnishings.[37]

That women might be working or contributing to the war effort in some way other than making do and mending is hardly apparent in this issue from 1941, already two years into the war. Most of the ads push household products, such as SCO (for cleaning ovens), Varene (for staining floors and furniture), Darkaline (another stain), and Japlac (a lacquer paint).[38] Only three ads in the entire issue—for Allenbury's Diet, Tampax, and a fruit salt—feature the faces of working military women.[39] There is a small ad for the WRNS, the women's corps of the Royal Navy, but the workers they need are decidedly domestic ones, cooks.[40] The largest feature on working has to do with organizing a bridge party to benefit the Red Cross or Evacuee Fund. Figuring out how to make the required tea sandwiches during rationing is the article's main focus.[41] Both the ad for the WRNS and this article suggest that woman's most important role as a wartime volunteer had to do with her cooking abilities, and that cookery was the way to winning the war. Although World War II disrupted traditional gender roles in some respects, giving some women the opportunity of crossing over into formally masculine occupations, the February 1941 issue of *Modern Woman* suggests that domestic ideology is still a strong force in women's lives.

Smith continued writing for *Modern Woman* after the war, until 1951, when another conservative backlash against women was already in full force. According to Summerfield, the conclusion of the war did not necessarily lead women to home and hearth, but the expectation existed that women should maintain traditional roles:

Increasingly in the 1940's psychologists contributed the authority of their view that children who were not mothered intensively during their first five years and possibly throughout their schooldays, would grow up suffering from all sorts of neurotic and psychopathological ills. . . . With, in addition, the panic about the birthrate in the 1940's, women were confronted with a powerful cluster of ideas urging them to give up work and go home. "Rearing babies through happy healthy childhood to independent maturity is even more important than wiring aeroplanes, and is a very much more absorbing and exacting task," wrote Gertrude Williams in *Women and Work* in 1945, sounding a typical note.[42]

For those women who had wired airplanes in World War II, the change was definitely abrupt, but it was also abrupt for women who had stayed at home during the war, since standards of mothering dramatically escalated. Not only did children need to be cared for, but they also required vast amounts of the mother's (not the parents') emotional energy. According to psychologist D. W. Winnicott, writing in 1957, the father's main responsibility was to stay alive and maintain the child's home. He recommended that the mother arrange a few outings with the father, thereby, as Janice Doane and Devon Hodges suggest, making even "[t]he father's relationship to the child . . . the responsibility of the mother."[43]

Domestic propaganda had its effect on women, whether they followed its dictates or not. Both those who stayed home and those who worked often experienced intense feelings of guilt, as is made evident in this memoir by a woman named Pauline Long:

The Government needed jobs for the returning heroes; women had to make their home and beautify them with feminine charm (up the birthrate). . . . Came demand feeding, babies inseparable from mothers on slings around our backs and fronts; came television, washing machines, and durable goods to make us feel wanted in the home. . . . Came Guilt—never think of yourself as a person, never have sex outside marriage, never never never leave your child, be content with Uncle Government's lovely domestic hardware. . . .[44]

Clearly, the payoff for women's renewed domesticity—the increase in consumer goods—was not enough for some women, and many felt bitter as they underwent the rapid changes from wartime to peacetime.

Both during and after the war, Stevie Smith's book page contradicted domestic values, instead advocating women's individuality and interests beyond the home. Far from distancing herself from mass media culture, as did many modernist writers, Smith was to enter into it, using her talent at irony and parody to alter, at least in the pages of *Modern Woman*, its emphasis. In this way, Smith helped to decenter domestic ideology from its dominant position, at least for some women readers. Her work in *Mod-*

ern Woman may not at first seem radical, but given the context in which it sits, perhaps it is even more radical than her experimental novels.

REVIEWS IN *MODERN WOMAN*, BOTH BEFORE AND AFTER THE WAR

Smith's book page fostered resistant reading by both undermining romantic/domestic plots and offering alternatives through other genres. Although she often reviewed and recommended romantic and domestic narratives, her absurd retelling of their plots completely undermines any endorsements she might make. Where the magazine's focus was narrow and constraining, Smith's was broad and all-encompassing: she included many more genres than are usually found on a woman's book page.

Of course, the success of both these techniques was dependent on a close relationship between reader and reviewer, since the women readers had to enjoy the in-joke of Smith's parodies, as well as trust her recommendations in other genres. Smith created this closeness by collapsing the distance between reviewer and reader through direct address. Her playful tone also suggested a closeness to the reader and an ability to confide in her, at the expense of the literary establishment. Parodic retellings pull readers into the joke, requiring their disruptive laughter.

The first of Smith's disruptive techniques, the use of parodic retelling, demands resistant reading in the manner suggested by Judith Fetterley in her classic *The Resisting Reader*. Fetterley claims that women are able to read against the grain of the dominating tradition, or read through an alternative angle of vision. The consequence of such a reading practice, according to Fetterley, "is that books will no longer be read as they have been read and thus will lose their power to bind us unknowingly to their designs."[45] Smith's reviews of romantic and domestic plots are themselves models of resistant reading, since they make invisible domestic ideology visible again through parody. But they are even more subversive in their fostering of resistant reading on the part of Smith's readers, who are encouraged through their amusement at her parodies to degrade accepted forms of reading. This dual resistance, on the part of both reviewer and reader, was made possible by Smith's use of the summary reviewing style, which proved to be a particularly handy weapon against domestic ideology, despite, or perhaps because of, its lack of acceptance in traditional reviewing circles.

According to Lindenberger, the summary style, which retells or emphasizes, is the least desirable of reviewing styles; he places it last in his hierarchical listing and pokes fun at it as an uncreative, plodding approach. After all, it has the effect of obscuring the reviewer's opinion or judgment, which he highly values.[46] However, Smith reveals in *Modern Woman* that the summary style is extremely effective in that it enables the reviewer to be both a presence and a nonpresence. On the one hand, Smith is very visible in these satiric retellings, since her ironic or playful voice is a cue that she finds these romantic and domestic plots absurd. On the other hand, Smith disappears in that she does not directly lecture the reader against romantic/domestic novels. Her choice of reviewing style says to her readers, "These novels are awfully funny; don't you find them that way too?" Thus, Smith structures her readers' responses, yet nevertheless enables her readers to make their own decisions in a way that the judgmental reviewing style could not. Smith shows us in these brief reviews that parodic retelling, normally associated with postmodern literature, can also be adapted to a postmodernist reviewing style, one that similarly collapses distance between reader and reviewer.

Smith's parodic reviews decenter domestic ideology by questioning its inherent values, thereby revealing that alternatives sets of values might exist beyond its boundaries. One of Smith's main assaults in these reviews is on the romantic and domestic notion that a girl must marry, no matter what the cost. Without directly saying so, Smith reveals that the costs of a poor choice in a husband are often extremely high and hardly worth the risk. Smith does not openly advocate unwedded life or the postponing of marriage until a woman has matured, but her reviews lead in that direction, since they mock plots in which bad marriages are easily resolved into happy ones.

For example, in her first issue, she recommends a romance entitled *Trailing Glory,* about a naive heroine who marries a card shark, yet undermines the girl's decision and, thus, the values of the book:

A girl is never too young to know that there are four aces to a pack of cards. But if you must marry a card-sharper, girls, see that he has a half brother who is the living spit of him in looks. Then, according to Ursula Bloom's entertaining new novel, *Trailing Glory . . . ,* you can switch over—and no questions asked. Perhaps. But we shall continue to teach our daughters that five aces to a pack spells trouble.[47]

Such a plot is not the stuff of life, Smith reminds us, and young girls need to be taught the dangers of marrying without thinking. Shrewdness is better than relying on one's husband's having a more suitable brother. But Smith's light tone, and her recommendation of the book for its entertainment value, suggest that the book's dangers may be indicated without harming either the reputation of the author, Ursula Bloom, or the self-esteem of women who enjoy these books. As in all her reviews, her comments tend to decenter the book's import. Read it, Smith suggests, but don't take it seriously, for as we both know, marriage is too important to handle with a flippant attitude that might carry over to the daughters of the next generation. In its general tolerance, her reviewing style mirrors that of the Victorian suffrage press, though it is unlikely Smith was familiar with their conventions.[48]

Another such example is the September 1941 review of Dorothy Cowlin's *Penny to Spend,* which similarly attacks the romance writer's inventiveness in leading the reader to a happy ending, even when the ending, according to Smith, was completely implausible:

Lovable people are often rather indecisive. Miss Dorothy Cowlin's heroine in *Penny to Spend* . . . is that sort of girl. The author shows her as a child, not knowing what to spend her penny on. Later in life the problem becomes more acute. Which man shall she marry? By an impossible device, plausibly conveyed (a tribute to the author's skill), Prunella is allowed to have her cake and eat it. Her first choice played out (in every sense), back go the hands of the clock, and there she is married to Prospect No. 2. Ladies who married Tom and sigh for Charles will follow Prunella's career with interest. Ladies who married neither Tom nor Charles may smile if they like.[49]

Again, this review comments on the importance of careful choice of one's marriage partner, suggesting that romance plots take it all too lightly. Having married neither Tom nor Charles, Smith would appear to be the one smiling at review's end.

Additionally, Smith attempts to decenter her reader's investment in the romance by revealing the inherent predictability in plots that supposedly promise excitement. Smith's ironic parodies would seem to say to a woman reader, "Surely you don't want to read this same old story again":

Our Geraldine takes on an ex-rich girl Elizabeth Vian as a maid. Geraldine is a wonderful fat loving girl who wants to make the best of herself. Elizabeth helps her. Then Tony Madison turns up and things get cockeyed. A. loves B., but B. loves C. There's also a fine new London shop. By Guy-Fletcher . . . , sure to be popular.[50]

Smith's last line seems to imply that it is only the setting (the fine new London shop) that is interesting in this story and that its plot is so well worn that its characters don't even need names, but can be labeled by letters. Her last comment—"sure to be popular"—encourages her readers to join her in being skeptical of popularity.

Another means by which she questions the preoccupation with the romance and the supposed excitement it brings is by making fun of its sham emotionality. Her mockery asks her woman readers, "Does romance really provoke as much excitement as these books suggest it does?" Smith's reviews frequently suggest that such emotionality is whipped up by authors:

My Enemy and I, by Theresa Charles . . . is one of those very long novels in which many delighted readers will lose themselves with the greatest of ease. The heroine is called Amoret Worplesdane (I am not making this up) and the Enemy, her enemy is Philip Grayle. "I wanted Philip to be mine. How, in enmity, friendship or love, I hadn't considered. All that mattered was that he should not remove himself from me," writes Amoret—who tells her own story. There is plenty of action in this book, and enough emotional steam to drive the Royal Scot to Edinburgh and back.[51]

When a book generates so much energy and emotionalism through romance, "enough to drive the Royal Scot to Edinburgh and back," perhaps that is too much energy invested in silliness, Smith suggests.

Most often, Smith's reviews gently question her readers' acceptance of romantic conventions through parody and through statements such as "some women readers will enjoy this" (the implication being that others might not) or "this book will no doubt be a bestseller" (even though others might not find it worthy of such attention). Smith's approach toward the popular novel differs greatly from that of modernists such as D. H. Lawrence, particularly in "Surgery for the Novel—or a Bomb." While she would have agreed with his call for the novel to represent "new feelings," as is evidenced by her own novels, she felt no need to "bomb" other writers out of existence.[52] Her parodies give her readers another context in which to view romantic works, one that suggests that these works' preoccupation with love and marriage (and their readers' subsequent investment in such a preoccupation) is not appropriate and natural, as *Modern Woman* itself suggests, but perhaps excessive and unnecessary. Such reviews encourage alternative thinking without setting up women readers in their traditional roles as passive receptors of knowledge. Smith's reviews suggest that it is as important to challenge women's passivity as readers as their preoccupations with love and romance.

However, such a reviewing style requires a great deal of restraint, since the author's voice and opinions are, to a certain extent, muffled. As the decade of the forties wore on, society's increasing conservatism and reliance on domestic ideology appear to have changed Smith's reviewing style somewhat. Smith is oftentimes less playful and more dogmatic in later reviews, as is evidenced in her review of Oriel Malet's *Miss Josephine and the Colonel:*

The early part where the children lose their parents in the San Francisco earthquake, and little Immaculata (of whom we get rather tired later) rounds them up and brings them to France on a wonderful trading ship is fine, but when they go and live with the aristocratic Colonel it smacks too much of feminine dreams and looking-glasses. The plot is preposterous.[53]

Here Smith is direct in her disgust at "feminine dreams." "Telling it slant" is never Smith's only rhetorical style, but rather only one technique among many.

In recognizing that new worlds must replace the old one of domestic ideology, Smith broadens her definition of the resistant reader beyond Fetterley's definition as one who reads against the grain. Smith was aware that any revisionary process involves going toward something as well as moving away from the undesirable. Therefore, she not only deconstructed domestic ideology through parodic retellings, but also encouraged women to escape from the boundaries of feminine fiction. She realized that women readers have often been ghettoized into reading from a too-narrow range of genres.

As Elizabeth Segel attests, women have been encouraged from childhood (since approximately 1850) to read a different set of books than males: "One of the most obvious ways gender influences our experience as readers is when it determines what books are made available to us or are designated as appropriate or inappropriate for our reading."[54] Though Claudia Nelson's work has modified our understanding of how and when this differentiation occurred, and Kate Flint has deepened our knowledge of what girls actually read (frequently "boy's" books rather than "girl's"), both acknowledge that children's reading material often worked to mark gender distinctions that were then reinforced in adults.[55] Smith frequently reviewed romantic/domestic fiction, associated with adult women readers, but she also included a wide variety of other genres: biographies, travel accounts, poetry, religious works, political and social treatises, and art books. Because the correspondence between Smith and Newnes has been lost, it is impossible to know exactly how much editorial control Smith had. But the recommendation of many of these books would seem to be her own choice, since the categories from which she chooses are those that most interested her throughout her life. Presumably, she wanted to share her own varied interests with the women readers of *Modern Woman*.

The most significant emphases in Smith's book pages were on works that directly counteracted prevailing ideologies of the time period, the emphasis on war and domesticity in the first half of the forties, the naturalness of home and family in the second half of the forties. Her book suggestions counteract the unified field of domestic ideology by suggesting, first of all, that war is far from the simplistic historical event that is portrayed in *Modern Woman*. She shows that it can be frightening as well as uplifting, and most important that its consequences require serious thought since winning the war will hardly lead to simple triumph and the resolution of all England's problems. The books she recommends in the second half of the decade question the opinions of prominent sociologists and psychologists on the naturalness of woman's place in the home. Theirs are not the only opinions, her recommendations would seem to say. In addition to merely opposing domestic ideology, her book recommendations open up many possible modes for women's and men's existence. *Modern Woman* readers are moved from the singularity of domestic ideology to a plurality of often conflicting and competing ideas. Thus, Smith's book pages endorse a world in which centrifugal forces overwhelm and decenter the single message of domestic centripetal force.

Far from encouraging the romantic view of the war, as manifested in Patricia Wentworth's 1941 story "Torpedo," Smith recommended books that show women acting in a variety of different war roles (not including being kissed on a burning deck). Some of these revealed the frustrating and tedious aspects of war, such as her friend Inez Holden's *Night Shift* (reviewed in February 1942), a novel about a week in the life of a woman munitions worker. Hardly romantic, the main character's life is characterized by exhaustion from the long hours and boredom with tedious, repetitive work. In addition, there are the food shortages and the very real dangers of getting home at dawn, when "Adolph's" planes are still flying. Recognizing that Holden's book hardly reveals views of women and war to which readers of *Modern Woman* are accustomed, Smith praises the book's honesty: "In its deceptively quiet way, it is probably as explosive as anything that ever came out of an ordnance factory."[56]

In recommending Holden's book, Smith was able to give her women readers a glimpse at "the other side" of the war, where some women were taking over traditionally masculine jobs. The job featured in Holden's book was that of a worker in the so-called industrial army. But women also worked in branches of the armed services, and Smith features their lives as well. In October 1942, she reviews an autobiographical account of an ATS worker, entitled *We Serve*. Smith recognizes that this book gives a much different account of ATS (Auxiliary Territorial Service) work than was commonly believed—the ATS was the least accepted women's corps during the war—and she heartily endorses the book's point of view:

We Serve, by R. M. Neill-Fraser . . . is a brave and cheerful account, written from personal experience of the life in the A.T.S. Prospective girl soldiers will be encouraged—and so will their parents.[57]

Smith's last line stops just short of encouraging young girls to join up, a position hardly endorsed by *Modern Woman*'s editors, who catered to married women, forgetting that these women might very well have younger daughters or know other unmarried women.

The number of autobiographies reviewed in Smith's book pages seems to indicate a desire to dilute romantic and domestic fiction with actual accounts by women and men who served in the war. She recommends not only those that tell of women in supportive roles back home, but also those of women involved in the fighting. In this way, she endorses an exhilarating and triumphant view of the war, as well as the depressing and frustrating one. But, most significantly, it is not the exhilaration to be gained vicariously, through romance. In October of 1941, for example, she recommends two autobiographies of women behind the lines, *Escape from France*, by Claire, and *Captured*, by Bessie Myers. These reviews are treated in the same paragraph, as they both tell the story of women who made their way from behind the lines to safety through their bravery. Smith admires their pluckiness and says so: "The courage of these girls is much the same; they had a perky sort of self-confidence which brought them through."[58]

Smith apparently felt that women readers also needed to know of men's experiences in the war, and therefore recommends males' accounts of the war. One of these is *What, No Morning Tea?* which tells of the first weeks in a recruit's life.[59] Although the tone of the book is light, it does reveal a man in the very unmasculine position of finding army life alien and strange. Here is no noble soldier bravely defending his country, but an ordinary person who is baffled by the changes in his life. Smith's advocacy of the book indicates that war is as lacking in romance for men as for the women left behind. She also recommends two far more specialized accounts of men and war, *The Last Enemy*, Richard Hillary's account of being an RAF pilot, and *Destroyer from America*, John Fernald's adventures in bringing over an American destroyer for use in the Royal Navy.[60] For women readers, these books would have destabilized their notions of war as simply a heroic and noble enterprise for men.

Perhaps Smith's most demanding suggestions during the war are an array of social and political books about the war, or the supposed aftermath of the war. Many times Smith does not agree with these writers' views, yet recommends them anyway. Although strongly opposed to Vera Brittain's pacifism, Smith includes her book *England's Hour* in the May 1941 issue.[61] In addition, she suggests H. G. Wells's *Guide to a New World* (Nov. 1941), Julian Huxley's *Democracy Marches* (Nov. 1941), and Sir Ernest Simon's *Rebuilding Britain—a Twenty Year Plan* (Apr. 1945).[62] Smith wants readers of *Modern Woman* not only to be familiar with the experiences of the war but also to consider why war occurs and what might be done to stop it. Smith gives her readers credit for being able to understand and process abstract argument as well as experiential accounts, credit that women readers do not receive in the rest of *Modern Woman,* since the magazine's focus is on getting women through the war and back to normalcy, not on questioning how the world fell out of normalcy in the first place.

After the war, Smith's book page challenges the increasing conservatism of attitudes toward women by including books that question the naturalness of traditional roles for women, such as intensive mothering and homemaking. For example, in April 1950 she reviews Margaret Mead's *Male and Female:*

[M]any of the patterns of masculine-feminine behaviour which the Western nations have come to think of as biological (that is, fixed in nature and of course "right") seem to be nothing more than an inherited tradition based on the "father" idea which is at the root of our culture. . . . It does one good to have one's mind refreshed by a book like this.[63]

Smith's parenthesis indicates that she is on Margaret Mead's side and questions what is considered right and proper for women.

She also recommends Doris Lessing's *The Grass Is Singing* in the June 1950 issue of *Modern Woman* for its heroine's stance on work:

Her novel is about a South African city girl, one of those odd girls who really are happier in an office with their girl friends than married and "with a home of their own."[64]

Her ironic use of the word odd and the quotation marks around "home of their own" suggest that Smith, as much as Lessing, is herself at odds with dominant fifties values. That Smith hopes other women will find such values similarly odd—and feel a need to bracket the culture's values—is indicated simply by her inclusion of the book, hardly reflective of the more typical *Modern Woman* fare.

While Smith endorses books by women such as Mead and Lessing, traditionalist books on gender roles receive short shrift, such as Richard Curle's *Women,* which Smith politely puts down for its "well-worn generalizations," finding it to be "more amusing than it is meant to be."[65] The brevity of this review and its mocking tone indicate that such traditionalist views are deserving of little time or commentary. Smith diminishes such values by giving them little space on her page; at least where she has control, they barely exist as a challenge.

As a reviewer for both popular women's magazines and the more prestigious literary magazines, Smith was, as in all her work, a crosser of boundaries. But in her reviews, Smith was unable to collapse the class and gender divisions of the reviewing world. After all, she was unable to completely reconfigure the literary world and was forced to work within its boundaries. However, even within those boundaries, her work confronts and disrupts a hierarchical literary world that largely confined women readers and producers to one genre while allowing men the freedom of all others. Such work should be considered feminist in its theoretical understanding and its pragmatic concern for women. As a woman reviewer, she often used her influence to get women novelists on the reviewing page, even though they sometimes did not like what she wrote. She thus broke down the division of spheres by her mere presence in those magazines, and the presence of the women writers she advocated. But perhaps more radically, she broke up the unrelieved domesticity of a magazine such as *Modern Woman* by not only offering women a wider selection of books but encouraging them to make their own decisions and have their own interests. Smith made herself a part of this women's sphere, thereby disturbing our notions of what is normally included in women's magazines and what counts as the popular. It would take another study to see if the women who read *Modern Woman* really did read Lessing or the Sitwells or any of Smith's other choices, but surely some of them must have "ferreted" out alternative narratives, or even if they did continue reading romances, they must have heard Smith's satiric retellings singing in their ears.

5

The Stories
1939, 1946–1955

Out of print since their first publication, Smith's ten short stories fortunately have been reissued in the Barbera and McBrien collection of miscellaneous writings entitled *Me Again* (1981). Of these, only "In the Beginning of the War" (1942), her one story published during the war, does not in some way concern domestic ideology. The remaining nine stories focusing on marriage and family were published either at the tail end of the interwar phase (1939), or after World War II, when their sardonic depictions of family life were greatly at odds with the centripetal forces of the culture. Far more savage in their tone than her novels, reviews, and many of her poems, Smith's stories need to be read as a response to continuing waves of conservatism.

After World War II, large numbers of women were laid off, nurseries were shut, and many hoped that "normal" family life, understood as depending upon a working father and a stay-at-home mother, would return again. During the war, women had been encouraged to view housework as a slapdash affair, exemplified by the "make do and mend" slogan; now they were exhorted to see "homemaking as a career," a job in itself.[1] Key figures in postwar reconstruction, women were given the responsibility of easing the psychological transition between war and peace. Margaret Stetz explains,

As in the nineteenth century, when wife and home were held by Victorian culture to be the reward earned by weary Empire-builders, so at the end of the Second World War, women were encouraged to subordinate their own wishes to those of the tired soldiers, who had been dreaming of domestic idylls past and future.[2]

Whether these women's "idylls" matched those of the returning soldiers was of lesser concern.

96

Why such ideological fervor developed is somewhat hard to understand, as women's labor was desperately needed in Britain's rebuilding efforts. Shortly after nursery subsidies were cut off (1946), the government again began recruiting women (1947), this time for the export production necessary to repay American loans.[3]

Certainly, there was anxiety over the birthrate, but the postwar baby boom quickly allayed these fears.[4] Concern was also generated by the increasing divorce rate and its potential effects on social order, but the dramatic rise, apparently caused by hasty wartime marriages and the strain of war, was balanced by a fall by the early fifties.[5] Nevertheless, domestic ideology was again in full force, promoted by a variety of sectors, left as well as right.

Far from disturbing traditional notions of the family, the postwar Labour government merely reinforced them. According to Elizabeth Wilson,

The welfare state was certainly perceived as supportive of family life, and was intended both to ease the lot of the breadwinner and to improve the situation of his dependants. Yet it supported this particular form of family life—a breadwinner and dependants—simply because no-one thought of any other way of doing things.[6]

As Wilson herself shows, the government's lack of imagination with regard to familial structure served a purpose, given that the family unit was expected to act as a stabilizing force during a time of other radical changes.[7]

Governmental views were further supported in academic arenas. Sociologists, psychologists, and mass media producers placed new emphasis on the importance of mothering, inextricably connected with traditional definitions of femininity. Functionalist sociology emphasized the "naturalness" of the traditional family, claiming that "all parts of the social organism were held to make their appropriate contribution," i.e., women were to stay in their "appropriate" place on the home front.[8] Psychologists in the Freudian tradition, such as John Bowlby and D. W. Winnicott, emphasized the necessity of intensive mothering, to the exclusion of fathering.[9] Strangely enough, these assumptions were rarely challenged, and feminism, hardly an organized movement in this period, was thought to have succeeded in its goals of offering equal opportunity to women.[10]

Although more and more women entered the workforce in this period, few saw themselves as professionals.[11] Even the literary career, one of the earliest professions open to women, was no longer easily accessible; as Alan Sinfield attests, "Writing was implicated in the attack on non-domesticity."[12] But while Sinfield blames restrictive ideology rather than market forces for shutting women out, Smith was to experience just the reverse: She continued writing yet had difficulty publishing.[13] Barbera and McBrien note that the short story largely preoccupied Smith during this period, but such a preoccupation appears to have been as much a necessity as a choice.[14] She was largely shut out of the poetry market, having had a hard time finding a publisher for her illustrated manuscript, *Harold's Leap* (1950), a difficulty that preoccupied her until after the publication of *Not Waving but Drowning* (1957). Fiction, traditionally a market more open to women, was only slightly more promising. Turned away from literary journals, her later short stories, sometimes commissioned by friends, appeared in venues aimed at more general audiences. No one knows exactly why Smith attempted suicide in 1953, but her shrinking literary possibilities surely cannot have helped her depression.

That Smith attributed her lack of success in this period to her position as a woman is documented in her correspondence with friend and fellow writer Naomi Mitchison, herself a feminist. In 1950, Smith wrote to Mitchison saying, "Truly I need a shover, a nice honey-tongued worm, to belly around for me, some pretty young man, eh? with a 'theory.'"[15] Smith's suspicion that she needed a male intermediary, when she had formerly been able to negotiate for herself, reflects her understanding that women were no longer as welcome in the literary marketplace, especially if they were older and "without theories." Smith was quickly finding herself unfashionable.

Though her fiction's caustic tone most likely intensified her difficulties, Smith was not alone in questioning cultural mandates on femininity. As Niamh Baker has shown, wholehearted acceptance of domestic life was by no means common among postwar women fiction writers: "What is interesting about the period is not just that so much of its fiction does represent marriage ambiguously, but that this ambiguity is not confined to the intellectual novel but permeates more popular fiction."[16] Baker suggests postwar women writers were better able to resist conservative constructions of femininity because of the long tradition of subversive writing they had to draw from.[17] Margaret Stetz supports her conclusions in an analysis of *The Ghost and Mrs. Muir* (1945), where she points out that Josephine Leslie (as R. A. Dick) rebelled against the "new feminine ideal" by turning to Forster, Shaw, "a comedy-of-manners tradition that looked back to Oscar Wilde," and the "New Woman" fiction of the 1880s and 1890s. As Stetz claims, there is an " 'inspiriting' potential [in] ghosts."[18]

The resistant methodology of Smith's short stories can be traced to her dialogue with American women satirists of the twenties and thirties, though Smith herself was ambivalent about such a distinctly American influence. Having read Dorothy Parker's stories in the mid-1930s when lent a copy by novelist Alice Ritchie, Smith had consciously mimicked Parker's rhythms in the writing of *Novel on Yellow Paper*. Twenty years later, however, she was embarrassed by the mannered style and the Americanisms of *Novel on Yellow Paper*, both of which she attributed to Parker.[19] Following her lead, Smith's critics have seen Parker's influence as an early one, limited largely to Smith's first novel.[20] In so doing, they have ignored Smith's short stories, which even more than her novels bear the mark of Parker and other American women satirists of the interwar period, such as Anita Loos, with whom Smith was also familiar.[21]

In adapting the linearity of Parker's and Loos's narratives, Smith's stories undermine romantic and domestic plots, and thus the institutions of marriage and family, through savage mimicry or retellings of traditional narratives rather than the dislocations and disruptions of experimental fiction. Using one form of resistance in her novels and another in her short stories, Smith anticipates Irigaray's rhetorical methods in *Speculum* by employing both what Irigaray calls "[o]verthrow[ing] syntax" (i.e., narrative dislocations) and what she calls "reimport[ing]" or "carry[ing] back" (i.e., parodic retellings).[22] It is in Smith's short stories that she was to "carry back" through a tradition of satire particular to early-twentieth-century women writers.

Of course, Smith was greatly attracted to the art of satire in general. The only book of literary criticism in her private collection is Humbert Wolfe's *Notes on the Art of Satire*.[23] In addition to Parker and Loos, she had read, as well as reviewed, Aldous Huxley and Evelyn Waugh, who also began their careers in the 1920s. Huxley was perhaps the earliest contemporary satirist Smith knew, as her private collection contains many of his earliest works: *Limbo* (1920), *Mortal Coils* (1922), *Antic Hay* (1923), *Along the Road* (1925), *Point Counterpoint* (1928), *Brief Candles* (1930), *Vulgarity in Literature* (1930), and *Eyeless in Gaza* (1936). Eventually, she was to review five of Huxley's works: *The Gioconda Smile* (1938), *After Many a Summer* (1939), *Grey Eminence* (1941), *Time Must Have a Stop* (1944), and *Ape and Essence* (1948).[24] Her interest in Evelyn Waugh came later: She collected *A Handful of Dust* (1934), *Put Out More Flags* (1942), *When the Going Was Good* (1946), and *The Loved One* (1948), and finally reviewed more of his works than Huxley's: *Scoop* (1938), *Put Out More Flags* (1942), *Work Suspended* (1942), *Brideshead Revisited* (1945), *Helena* (1950), *Men at Arms* (1952), and *Officers and Gentlemen* (1955).[25] Yet, Huxley's and Waugh's influence is largely an indirect one, since Smith's satire works in opposition to theirs, most particularly when the topic is gender.

Smith and her fellow women satirists lack the basic identifying trait of Huxley's and Waugh's works: nostalgic longing. Despite very different political allegiances, Huxley and Waugh both attribute social disorder to the same problem: changing gender roles. As Sandra Gilbert and Susan Gubar have already claimed with respect to Huxley, many male writers during this period were increasingly anxious about women's literary potential.[26] That they should choose satire as their genre seems hardly a coincidence. According to John Snyder in *Prospects of Power*, satire is particularly suited to a period of social change, since "[t]he satiric impulse wilts when there is a domineering political consensus."[27] It is no wonder that the decade of the twenties, following the gains of women during World War I, marks such an active period in satire by both male and female writers, though it is largely the male names that we have remembered.

Both Huxley and Waugh blame women for reconfiguring power relationships much to the detriment of male-female interaction, and long for a "righting" of gender roles, for what they see as a return to normalcy. Huxley's *Limbo*, Smith's first introduction to his work, serves as a case in point. *Limbo*'s lead story, "Richard Greenow," has been previously cited by Gilbert and Gubar as an example of male literary defensiveness, since Dick Greenow's writing is feminized, and thus weakened in quality, through his "possession" by the spirit of Pearl Bellairs, a romantic novelist.[28] But "Richard Greenow" also serves as a "warning story," much like those in Pearson publications of the twenties, cautioning society against further disruption in traditional gender roles. In a reversal of expected roles, it is Greenow's sister Millicent who is the efficient military organizer, while Greenow remains a pacifist (as Dick) and a jingoistic writer (as Pearl). That such a state is intended to be seen as perverse and unnatural is made clear by Dick's madness and eventual death; men's literal survival, it would seem, is dependent on a return to traditional gender roles.[29]

If possible, Waugh's nostalgia is even more direct. In *A Handful of Dust*, which Smith had also read, it is Tony Last's wife, Brenda, who ends the happiness of the household because of her longing to leave the isolated life of their country estate and possibly even pursue an economics degree. Waugh contrasts Tony and Brenda's "modern" marriage with that of Tony's parents, who represent a more traditional, and apparently much happier, way of life. Tony's parents companionably shared the Guinevere room of their Gothic castle, as opposed to their son and daughter-in-law, who occupy separate bedrooms and, finally, separate houses. The unraveling of Tony and Brenda's marriage comes about, predictably, because of Brenda's increasing independence and curiosity about the world beyond the family.[30] Both Waugh's and Huxley's works end tragically, as, of course, the past cannot be recaptured.

But for the women satirists under discussion, the past offered no answer to male-female relationships. For them, marriage and gender relations remained predictably the same (too much a continuation of the past). In their writing, marriage is seen as leading to women's isolation and lack of voice, as women continue to have little financial or psychological independence in marriage. Parker's and Loos's narratives, therefore, act as assaults on the nostalgic warning stories of Huxley and Waugh, as well as on traditional romantic and domestic plots, since their retelling of these plots exposes domesticity's horrors. In using satire to expose the problematic aspects of marriage at a later date, Smith's short narratives echo their diatribes.

Yet, Smith's narratives differ from Parker's and Loos's in one significant way: their endings. No mere imitator of her satiric foremothers, Smith was to join them in a dialogue on the divisiveness of male-female relations and the possibilities for changing a society structured around gender opposition. In this dialogue, it is Smith who is more radical, since her stories demolish domesticated worlds, or, more commonly, offer options for reconfiguring society. On the other hand, Parker's and Loos's narratives typically dead-end in a lament on current conditions. Parker, failing to see any change possible in gender relations, adopts the tragic endings common to Waugh or Huxley, while Loos simply avoids an end to Lorelei the gold digger's story. Although Parker and Loos do not like the way the world is configured, they appear powerless to change it. According to the definitions of Nancy Walker in *A Very Serious Thing: Women's Humor and American Culture*, their satire should be viewed as feminist in that it exposes the falseness of stereotypes, in this case the "bliss" of marriage and family life, yet it should be differentiated from Smith's type of feminist humor that "more overtly confronts the source of discrimination."[31]

Hardly powerless, Smith's endings resist patriarchal ideology through gradually becoming more fantastic. As Walker has claimed, the more radical type of feminist humor frequently relies on fantasy to reenvision women's state.[32] While the early endings of Smith's stories merely act as anarchistic, Menippean rejections of societal values, her post–World War II stories often end happily, with some third party entering to solve the situation. Though seemingly realistic, it is the suddenness and implausibility of these happy endings that make them fantastic. Through this vault from satire to fantasy, Smith was to capitalize on the basic instability of satire.

As John Snyder suggests, satire must blend with another genre in order to reach resolution:

[S]atire is a semigenre only, a genre that stops itself from becoming a fully distinct alternative to other genres. . . . It is unstable as a genre in that it must detour around its perplexity about human nature by constantly seeking its resolutions outside itself, by subordinating itself to being a mode coloring or supplementing other, more dominant genres, especially tragedy and the novel, and, in return, acquiring color or determination from them.[33]

According to Snyder, satirists resolve their dilemmas in one of three ways:

Satiric irony ends up either leaning back toward the nonevaluative and absolute solutions of action-based tragedy, or turning forward toward the developmental ontology fully possible only in the realist novel of the eighteenth and nineteenth centuries, and later, in the self-conscious fiction of the twentieth century. Or satiric irony may yearn entirely away, toward the freedom from all rational rule that has always been possible through fantasy. . . .[34]

As in previous works, Smith was to employ a crossing of art forms as a means of reconfiguring conservative ideologies. Unable to accept what Snyder has called the "nonevaluative" ending of tragedy, she was to cross the deflating tendencies of satire with the more comic characteristics of fantasy.[35] This combination enabled her simultaneously to deconstruct the second wave of domestic ideology and offer alternative social patterns. In this respect, her later stories resemble her last novel, *The Holiday,* with its "new" rhythms. Perhaps challenged by the increasingly conservative society surrounding her, Smith is at her most visionary in her work from the end of the war to the mid-fifties.

WOMEN'S INTERWAR SATIRE

For Parker, Loos, and Smith, narratives of traditional domesticity hid or obscured the inherent problems of marriage and family, particularly for women. Opposing those who would reassure women of their eventual contentment in married life, these women writers develop three major criticisms of domesticity: (1) it isolates women in the home; (2) it robs women of their voice and identity; and (3) it puts them in a dangerous position of economic dependence. As retellings of Parker's and Loos's narratives, themselves satiric retellings of domestic ideology, Smith's short stories repeat their concerns, using their early critiques against later, and more severe, waves of domestic ideology. Rather than attempting to disrupt the linearity of the traditional domestic narrative, Parker, Loos, and Smith use linearity against itself by "replaying" the traditional narratives, distorting them beyond recognition.

Hardly a state of romantic intimacy, marriage, for Parker, is a condition of isolation that grows increasingly frightening rather than increasingly satisfying. Separated from any true communication by their divided gender roles, Parker's couples have nothing to say to each other. For example, the newlyweds in "Here We Are" are not married for more than a few minutes before they discover the gulf between them:

"Well!" he said. "Well. How does it feel to be an old married lady?"

"Oh, it's too soon to ask me that," she said. "At least—I mean. Well, I mean goodness, we've only been married about three hours, haven't we?"

The young man studied his wrist-watch as if he were just acquiring the knack of reading time.

"We have been married," he said, "exactly two hours and twenty-six minutes."

"My," she said. "It seems like longer."[36]

The title of the story—"Here We Are"—becomes a repeated refrain that expresses their inability to converse and their growing awareness that marriage itself brings no automatic connection, despite the promises of women's magazine narratives.

Such lack of communication is particularly devastating for the women in Parker's stories, since they, as stay-at-home, middle-class wives, are totally dependent on their husbands for companionship. Grace in "Too Bad" does nothing all day except buy flowers and try to string the mundane events of the day into lively conversation. Because she has a maid, her work around the house is limited to providing what she considers the feminine touches essential to a marriage, i.e., moving the flower vases around in an effort to give her flat a homey, domesticated look. Driven to discussions of tomato soup and rhubarb pie, the topics that dinner supplies, she wonders what is wrong with her relationship, and thus allows Parker's readers to discover that the rapt, silent nature of romantic thralldom is merely a sign of communicative lack:

She tried to remember what they used to talk about before they were married, when they were engaged. It seemed to her that they never had had much to say to each other. But she hadn't worried about it then; indeed, she had felt the satisfaction of the correct, in their courtship, for she had always heard that true love was inarticulate. Then, besides, there had been always kissing and things, to take up your mind. But it had turned out that true marriage was apparently equally dumb. And you can't depend on kisses and all the rest of it to while away the evenings, after seven years.[37]

The irony of the story is that the Weldons do, as their friends say, "[get] along so beautifully together," in that they are scrupulously polite, but that is simply not enough.[38] Her inexperience of the public sphere and his lack of interest in the private sphere's domestic details leave them completely estranged. For Parker, the very basis of traditional marriage, its division of gender roles, is what ensures its eventual collapse.

Anita Loos also points out the estrangement and loneliness of marriage, although more comically. In *But Gentlemen Marry Brunettes,* the sequel to *Gentlemen Prefer Blondes,* gold digger Lorelei is married to the wealthy Henry Spoffard, whose money alone holds her interest. She justifies her movie career (a hobby rather than a means of support) on the grounds that it improves their marriage:

> . . . I think that practically every married girl ought to have a career if she is wealthy enough to have the home life carried on by the servants. Especially if a girl is married to a husband like Henry. Because Henry is quite a homebody and, if a girl was a homebody too, she would encounter him quite often. . . . So I am practically always picking up something, and then when I go back and encounter Henry, I always have some new remark, or other, to make. . . . And it is bright ideas that keep the home fires burning. . . .[39]

The irony of Lorelei's rationalizations is that she avoids Henry because they share no interests: Their occasional encounters are hardly stimulating enough to "keep the home fires burning." As estranged as Grace and Jim in "Too Bad," Henry and Lorelei are just less self-aware and have a greater tolerance for boredom.

Neither as tragic as Parker's nor as comic as Loos's, Smith's stories nevertheless retell, or expose, their concern with marriage's isolation and boredom. However, Smith's often lower-middle-class marriages are characterized, paradoxically, both by isolation and togetherness. Cut off from the world and eventually from their husbands, Smith's wives are as bored and weary as those of Parker's stories, yet they are also frustrated by continual contact between family members with whom they have no real intellectual or spiritual connection.

A large part of Peg's unhappiness in "The Herriots" (1939) is that she cannot escape the family sphere, exemplified by continual contact with her in-laws. As her situation with her husband worsens, she has a nightmare that links her marital claustrophobia with that of other suburban families:

> She was walking along and round. She knocked at all the doors down a long street, at each door there was a woman who answered the bell. There was no conversation between them, only gestures. A refusal, and the door was closed. Inside each house there were little rooms. The rooms were the homes of the people. There were old ladies and gentlemen, nodding on separate chairs; there were young married couples with babies, the babies were crying, the women were laughing sometimes and talking with their husbands; sometimes they were silent and angry.[40]

Here Smith's metaphor of the dominant social structure is a rat maze, each family confined to their own isolated rat hole, with no outside interests.

This vision of continual isolation and yet continual togetherness horrifies Peg, for it is a vision of her own life reflected in that of others.

Smith's later stories, after the war, are equally bleak. The family in "Beside the Seaside" quarrel over trivial matters because they seldom engage with anyone else. One of the few happy moments in the story occurs when the father, Henry, makes a joke about someone else's family, and thereby forgets his obsessive concern with himself and his family.[41] Glory in "Sunday at Home" is unhappy because her husband's life offers him stimulating contact with outsiders, while she is supposed to stay at home and do housework: "I love Ivor, I never see him, never have him, never talk to him, but that the science is wrapping him round."[42] She finds her domestic life totally uninteresting:

She picked up the french beans and began to slice them. Now it would have to be lunch very soon. And then some more washing up. And Mrs. Dip never turned up on Friday. And the stove was covered with grease.[43]

Although she has more to do than the vase-moving Grace in Parker's "Too Bad," Glory is equally depressed, since a steady routine of cutting the French beans leaves her bored, and boring to her husband, who entertains himself with his female research assistants.

Through this boredom and isolation, as well as their treatment by their husbands, the wives of these stories lose all voice or identity. Whereas the traditional domestic plot portrays romantic union as the happy melding of two beings, Parker, Loos, and Smith reveal marriage to be a relationship in which the husband's personality dominates and the wife's eventually disappears. Their critique of women's voicelessness also ends up challenging the hierarchical arrangement of traditional marriage, which continually gives the male more power in the relationship.

In Parker's "Glory in Daytime," Mr. Murdock shows no interest in his wife's enthusiasm for an upcoming visit with a famous movie star. Failing to see her boredom and her desperate need for any human contact, he is oblivious to her new interest as a revelation of personality:

. . . and Hallie Noyes said to me, "Come on in to tea tomorrow. Lily Wynton's going to drop up," she said. "Just like that, she said it. Just as if it was anybody."

"Drop up?" he said. "How can you drop up?"

"Honestly, I don't know what I said when she asked me. . . ."

"You might ask her how she'd like to try dropping down, for a change," Mr. Murdock said.

"All right, Jim," Mrs. Murdock said. "If that's the way you want to be."

Wearily she went toward the door, and this time she reached it before she turned to him. There were no lights in her eyes.[44]

An interrupted wife is a common occurrence in Parker's stories, as the wife in "Mr. Durant" never manages to make a case for keeping the family dog since her husband continually cuts her off, having already made up his mind that the dog is to go.[45] Parker reveals a pattern of wives steadily growing more timorous and unable to speak coherently since they have never been allowed to do so.

While Parker's husbands stall all conversation, Loos's males encourage Lorelei to speak, but they equally silence any real expression on Lorelei's part. When Lorelei talks, both her boyfriend and her eventual husband fail to hear the reality of what she says. Although Lorelei has no literary interests, they see her as an artistic person and a reader:

Well I forgot to mention that the English gentleman who writes novels seems to have taken quite an interest in me, as soon as he found out that I was literary. . . . [H]e has sent me a whole complete set of books for my birthday by a gentlemen called Mr. Conrad. They all seem to be about ocean travel although I have not had time to more than glance through them. I have always liked novels about ocean travel ever since I posed for Mr. Christie for the front cover of a novel about ocean travel by McGrath because I always say that a girl never really looks as well as she does on board a steamship, or even a yacht.[46]

So enamored are they of her appearance, and so content with her appearance alone, that they project a character onto her. Whatever kind of woman they desire is the woman Lorelei becomes, so that Gerry Larson, the novelist, imagines her a novelist also. Eventually Lorelei becomes engaged to a religious husband who finds her to be the prototypical "nice" girl. Never really listened to, Lorelei remains a chameleon character who changes with each man.

Smith's portrayal of married interaction and its effect on women is closer to Parker's in that she exposes marriage's destruction of a woman's identity and development. Peg from "The Herriots" has no voice in her mother-in-law's house, cannot even put up her own seersucker curtains, and finds it increasingly difficult to confront her husband about his irresponsible behavior. Unable to deny him anything, she ends up giving him their last bit of money to finance his fun-fair scheme, which of course fails, leaving them and the baby without food or coal. For Smith, losing one's voice comes close to losing one's existence.

Several of Smith's later stories portray husbands who appear more interested in their wives than is Peg's husband Coke, but really only desire a dominant position, no matter how little that dominant position means in terms of real power. When the unmarried Lisa, from "A Very Pleasant Evening," asks her friend Helen about her children, Helen's husband interrupts with a patronizing lecture on kangaroos. Helen's and Anita's husbands quickly become involved in a heated debate over kangaroos, which neither really knows anything about:

> The sea mouse, said Helen's husband, and began to talk about the kangaroo and the young kangaroo that is, he said, born a worm. How can that be, said Lisa, a worm. No the kangaroo, it is like this, he is born with his claws and his fur on, but he is not quite finished off yet for all that, so the mother puts the child kangaroo into her pouch . . . or poosh, said Roland rather irritatingly.[47]

This pattern of trying to achieve verbal victories occurs all evening, Roland later taking over the conversation with literary quotations, to the exclusion of the wives' voices and the relative exclusion of the unmarried Lisa's voice. In "Beside the Seaside," Helen and Margaret's seaside conversation is also interrupted by Margaret's husband Henry, who pontificates on the Russians' possession of the atom bomb.[48] Smith eventually reveals that these patterns of domination extend even beyond marital boundaries, affecting all women. In "The Story of a Story," Helen's writing of a story about Bella and Roland is prevented by Roland's anger.[49] Thus, a woman's voicelessness carries over into the literary sphere, where she can be publicly silenced.

Through her exposure of these dominating maneuvers, Smith shows that a hierarchy quickly gets set up in a marriage, with a husband's information receiving more merit. The wives in her stories lose the thread of conversation with their women friends by trying to give credence to the topics and opinions of their husbands, as absurdly out of place as they may be, with the result that they express less personality than do their unmarried counterparts. Significantly, Parker and Loos never present a counterpart to their married characters; in their stories gender patterns are all-encompassing. Hardly to be admired, they are somehow unable to be changed. Their stories, therefore, make women appear unintelligent and inarticulate. Smith's, on the other hand, reveal this inarticulateness to be more clearly a function of domesticity itself.

But for all their jibes at marriage, Parker, Loos, and Smith are at their most savage over what they consider the worst aspect of domesticity: the financial dependence of women on men. While the traditional domestic romance presents marriage as a relationship of security and comfort for women, the three women satirists show marriage as leading only to dependency and desperation. Parker's "Big Blonde" is one of her most terrifying and pathetic stories. Its heroine, Hazel Morse, finds marriage to be anything but secure. After her alcoholic husband leaves her, she cycles through financial dependence on man after man, unable even to remember their names. That Hazel has no idea of any other way to lead her life is made clear by Parker at the beginning of the story:

Men liked her, and she took it for granted that the liking of many men was a desirable thing. Popularity seemed to be worth all the work that had to be put into its achievement. . . .

No other form of diversion, simpler or more complicated, drew her attention. She never pondered if she might not be better occupied doing something else.[50]

Hazel's inability to be better occupied leads to alcoholism, prostitution, and finally suicide, despite her first marriage, which was supposed to promise her stability for life.

Anita Loos's Lorelei is a more lucky version of Hazel; she cycles through men, but eventually ends up with the stable and wealthy husband, the supposed prize of domestic ideology. The entire story centers on Lorelei's recognition of her dependence and her willingness to do anything to ensure her security. Lorelei appears manipulative and ruthless, which she is, but her behavior is motivated by a desire to avoid Hazel's fate, her one attempt to support herself having ended in harassment and a murder charge.[51] Loos exposes that even the happy ending to the romance plot, which Hazel was denied, is anything but happy, as Lorelei is completely dependent and married to a man she cares little about.

Smith's main story dealing with a married woman's vulnerability is "The Herriots," which Barbera and McBrien, because of the character's name and because of the many autobiographical details, see as a nightmarish projection of the way Smith's life might have gone if she had married.[52] Peg's husband skips from job to job, leaving his family more and more desperate. Never even thinking of a job of her own until later in the story, Peg is completely dependent on him for her and her baby's support. In later stories, Smith's married women are better off, but equally as dependent and desperate. Glory, from "Sunday at Home," tries to leave her husband the scientist, only to return for an unspecified reason, most likely her recognition of her inability to survive by herself.

Parker's, Loos's, and Smith's stories can all be considered feminist in that they disrupt conventional views of married women and to a certain extent expose the social conditions that create dependent, inarticulate women. Yet Parker's and Loos's stories are finally less feminist in their lack of sympathy for the women they portray; they fail to see themselves as connected to these women, in effect claiming a social "outside" where some women (themselves), by virtue of talent and intelligence, are exempted from the "normal" woman's inadequacies. They are thus finally limited in their ability to see the ways in which gender roles confine and constrain all women. On the other hand, Smith's writing acknowledges the pain of women who mindlessly walk through their social roles, even when they appear silly or misguided. Peg in "The Herriots" has made a bad marriage, but Smith empathizes with her trapped condition:

Peg had nowhere to go to get away from them. She wandered round the house distraught. She looked into the sitting room, old Mr. Herriot was reading his paper. Mrs. Herriot was in their room, looking for something. Peg went into the scullery (they had no maid now) and began to do the vegetables for dinner. She began to cry; now that she was alone she could think again.[53]

The fact that Smith depicted herself as one of these married women shows an understanding of the ways in which society's ideology has the ability to affect all women. Not wanting to take that imaginative risk, Parker and Loos always keep a certain distance between themselves and their characters.

Having thoroughly demolished the illusions of the traditional domestic world, these women writers are nevertheless pessimistic about any hope for a quick change of social institutions. One of satire's possible endings, as seen above, is the leap into the ontological possibilities of the realistic narrative, but there is little hope in any of these women's stories that such change could be expected to occur. In fact, any visible changes merely replay the old order. For example, Ivor's female research assistants in Smith's "Sunday at Home" care for him in the public sphere, as Glory does in the private; they may be scientists, but they are still primarily emotional caretakers. Such pessimism leads Smith to fantasy, a genre choice that suggests change is possible, but only through extreme imaginative leaps. Smith's stories argue that the psychological pull of the family is so great that only abrupt reordering, not small incremental changes, can lead to a different world.

ANARCHISM AND FANTASY

The endings of two of Smith's earliest stories, "Surrounded by Children" (1939) and "A Very Pleasant Evening" (1946), propose no more of an alternative to the domestic narrative than do Parker's and Loos's, yet these stories are finally more defiant in that Smith explodes social conventions with grotesque, even violent endings. Using the anarchistic tradition of Menippean satire, which provides "a definitive rupture between the rotten past and brand-new future," Smith shocks the reader into a revulsion against the pull of domestic ideology.[54] Her goal is not mere disruption but the destruction of the society she depicts.

One such story, and perhaps the best example, is "Surrounded by Children," Smith's second published story. It opens on a scene in Kensington Gardens, where mothers watch their children, and specifically their daughters, care for their sons/brothers. In focusing on their responsibility, Smith emphasizes that domesticity leads to women's role as selfless caretakers: "The brothers of the sisters and the babies of the mothers have no care at all; theirs is a careless fate, to be pampered and cared for. . . ."[55] For Smith, this caretaking exemplifies not generosity and benevolence, but the exhaustion of these women and the final loss of identity.

However, Smith does not leave her story with these women resigned to their fate, as does Parker. Into this proper domestic scene walks an elderly woman, whom Smith calls a "famously ugly old girl," and who disrupts the entire scene. According to Mary Russo in "Female Grotesques: Carnival and Theory," old women, like pregnant women and women with "irregular bodies," act as grotesques in that they defy social definitions of what women should be.[56] Russo sees their entrance as "unruly when set loose in the public sphere."[57] Smith's famously ugly old girl does indeed prove unruly, as she literally stops the actions in Kensington Gardens with the spectacle of her body.

Deciding to climb into the soft berth of an empty pram, and thus drawing the attention of those in the park, the old woman becomes a sign that combats domestic ideology. Lying in the carriage, she acts as a parodic symbol of both babyhood and motherhood. Hardly the attractive, cuddly baby that the domestic narrative presents, she is the nightmare baby, an ugly representation of what the mother eventually produces: death, not life. (This is not the only story in which Smith contests the domestic illusion of the perfect child, as the children in "Getting Rid of Sadie" are potential murderers.)[58] Pricked on her hatpin, the old woman bleeds onto the white frills of the pram in a parodic retelling of birth. She is an emblem of woman past her prime, old and used up, and thus a warning sign to all women. Of course, as Jack Barbera suggests, this woman may represent Smith's nightmarish fears of herself as an undesirable, unmarried woman, a sign that Smith was affected by the pressures of domestic ideology.[59] Yet the final effect of this woman is the disruption of the smooth flow of social interaction—and the narrative.

After all, the sight of the woman's body entices the park visitors to leave their normal domestic tasks and indulge in a parody of the domesticity they themselves represent. Their communal laughter, what Bakhtin would call "carnival laughter," disrupts the social order: "[T]his laughter is ambivalent: it is gay, triumphant, and at the same time mocking, deriding. It asserts and denies, it buries and revives."[60] Burying the remnants of their social selves, the people's laughter allows subversion to surface, thus ending, at least momentarily, the placid social order of Kensington Gardens.

Almost as anarchistic is the ending of the later "A Very Pleasant Evening," where a single woman visits two married couples, only to have the evening end on a strange, and somewhat frightening, note. The visit itself appears uneventful, even banal. Lisa tries to talk to her school friend, only to have their interaction interrupted by the two husbands. Such domineering action appears normal to all the women concerned. Even the unmarried Lisa plays along with the husbands' behavior until the end of the evening.

Yet Smith eventually connects this seemingly normal subordination of woman, which all the women in the story take for granted, with a later moment, where the subordination of women takes on a darker cast. One of the husbands, Roland, walks Lisa to the subway stop, only to kiss her, holding her in a "furious adroit grip."[61] As in many of Smith's poems, the potential for violence against women lurks just beneath the surface, often dissipating into normalcy, as it does in this story. Roland does not hurt Lisa, and she seems to enjoy the kiss, claiming, as she leaves, that she had a very pleasant evening. That Lisa does not question the kiss or appear to mind it is one of the more unsettling aspects of the story. The fierce kisses at the end of the story explode the normalcy of the previous domestic scene, Roland's brief infidelity, and Lisa's acceptance of it, opening up new questions to a reader. Romantic passion is linked to violence rather than love, and marriage is revealed not to be secure or safe.

After these destructive endings, Smith was to leave satire behind, finally experimenting with the fantastic. Some of these endings are blatantly fantastic in their resolutions; for example, Peg's situation in "The Herriots" is resolved by a dream. Most others, however, are seemingly more realistic. What makes them fantastic is, first of all, their implausibility, since Smith's stories often move quickly from tension and distress to peaceful contentedness. But even more important, these endings signal a subtle move away from domestic patterning. According to Brian Attebery, in *Strategies of Fantasy,* fantasy's escapism need not necessarily involve a recognizably unreal world: "Fantasy is a sophisticated mode of storytelling characterized by stylistic playfulness, self-reflexiveness, and a subversive treatment of established orders of society and thought."[62] The social patterns envisioned in Smith's endings, which definitely subvert "established orders," can be compared to those described in Rachel Du-Plessis's analysis of contemporary speculative fiction.

DuPlessis finds that instead of focusing on an individual or a couple, these woman writers establish what she calls a "collective protagonist," or a narrative world structured around nonfamilial groups.[63] DuPlessis, who sees these texts as restructuring the narratives by which we know ourselves, calls this narrative technique "the poetics of estrangement," since these new endings lead to a questioning of normalcy.[64] Smith was to create her own poetic estrangement by leading her readers from the supposed normalcy of intimate family contact to the opening up of family life through the entrance of others.

In "Beside the Seaside," Smith suggests that groups formed by women friends can act as powerful antidotes to domesticity. Although the story opens on the unmarried friend Helen visiting a family, Helen is quickly pulled into the suffocating emotionality of family life. However, the women—Margaret, her daughter Anna, and Helen—eventually "escape" in friend Phoebe's car. No chance journey, this is portrayed by Smith as a subversive act:

"It is an escape," she said, "an escape from the men." (From Hughie, she thought, from the restless son, the troubled father.) "Hurrah. A car full of women is always an escaping party. . . . The boiled mutton is forgotten, the care of the children, the breadwinner's behest, the thought for others; it is an escape."[65]

Not only an escape for the women, it is an escape for the narrative, as it breaks the focus on the family. And for Helen, that break remains permanent for the rest of the story. Margaret must eventually go back to her furious son and husband, but Helen simply departs, as though there is no difficulty in leaving behind the whole overemotional, domestic mess. In ending with Helen anticipating a quiet mussel supper with Phoebe, Smith's story reveals that it is possible literally to walk away from the culture, though that movement involves a complete break with the past, as the field between Margaret/Henry and Phoebe acts as a kind of no-man's-land between two entirely different worlds. In crossing the bridge that leads to Phoebe's world, Helen crosses into an escapist sphere, resembling the beach world of Margaret and Henry only in that there are mussels in both.

Although "Beside the Seaside" does champion the abandonment of men through a collective of women, the endings of Smith's stories are not usually so misandric. In fact, Smith's prose often concentrates on the ways in which men and women might relate to each other in new ways not dependent on dominant-subordinate configurations. As in *The Holiday*, one solution she suggests is "the rhythm of friendship," societal interaction based on the relationship between friends and more distant relations, such as uncles and cousins.[66] These stories are further tied to *The Holiday* in that she makes use of the same characters, such as cousin Caz, even though they may be given different names.

The story "Is There a Life beyond the Gravy?" replays the plot of *The Holiday* in that Celia, Cas, and Tiny go off on a country visit to Uncle Heber's; as in *The Holiday*, Uncle Heber's country estate is located as a place of escape, first through the characters' childlike regressions, finally through their "death." Celia, Cas, and Tiny seem to grow younger as the story continues; Uncle Heber even talks of their being on vacation from school, when at the beginning of the story they were working as responsible adults at the ministry. Yet despite their transformation into children or ghosts, Celia, Cas, and Tiny are finally more content at Uncle Heber's. The intruder who threatens to break them up, Clem in *The Holiday*, Augustus here, is chased away by the loyal three, who declare that they prefer being on the other side, even if the other side represents death.[67]

What sets apart this other world is the free and easy relations of Celia, Cas, and Tiny, so different from the interactions of her stories' married couples. The equality between the three friends contrasts with their hierarchical relationships with Lord Loop (Augustus) and, to a lesser extent, Celia and Tiny's employer, Sir Sefton. That Lord Loop and Sir Sefton suggest the "other" world of hierarchies is indicated by their titles, since no other characters are aristocrats. They also exchange a dead hare, another sign that they function in a dominant-subordinate world rather than the escapist, antihierarchical world that women and animals often share in Smith's poems.[68] Whenever Lord Loop and Sir Sefton intrude, they threaten the alternative world by bringing a world of hierarchical relations with them, exemplified later in the story by school life. Smith was to see school, like religion, as one of the ultimate expressions of hierarchy, in its "grading" of an individual's progress through structured levels.[69] Yet Celia, Cas, and Tiny persist in their championing of nonhierarchical life, since Celia asserts that they have no need of school: they know enough without it. Leaving behind the adult world of rationality, Smith takes us into an irrational world, not of childhood per se, since Celia, Cas, and Tiny are not really children, but a world that is outside the boundaries of both childhood and adulthood, as well as life and death.

"To School in Germany" ostensibly concerns World War II, yet like *The Holiday* connects the politics of nations with gender politics: It suggests that the choice of democracy over fascism is also the choice of the rhythm of friendship over hierarchical domestic rhythms. Recounting the story of her romance with a young German boy to her cousin Eustace (Caz/Cas), the unnamed female protagonist sees her old boyfriend Maxi enter the cafe, only to have Eustace recognize him, and arrest him, as a Nazi war criminal. Maxi's Nazi violence is tied to his view of all personal interactions, since he tried to bully the protagonist, as a young girl, into marrying him:

I was going to walk off aloofly and get the picnic things out when Maxi leapt at me. "Don't you know I love you?" . . .

... I stopped because of the way Maxi was looking. "I say, you aren't serious, I suppose? I say, look out, you'll break my arm."

He got a grip on my plaits and pulled my head back. "I say, look out, you're pulling my hair. Maxi do shut up."[70]

Maxi's world represents one of domination, while Eustace's world, the preferable alternative world, is one of egalitarian freedoms.

The literal break between the two stories, that of Maxi and that of Eustace, acts to disconnect the world of Maxi from that of Eustace, and thus acts, as does the open field in "Beside the Seaside," as the delineation between worlds. The female protagonist's "choice" of Eustace over Maxi is not only a personal choice but also a political choice, in that it signifies a desire for a world structured differently than Maxi's. That this connection between the personal and the political was intentional on Smith's part is made clear by the fictional changes she makes in what is basically an autobiographical story. Smith was once in love with a young German-speaking Swiss boy named Karl, but he was no Nazi. Her transformation of Karl into Maxi indicates that she wanted to make an explicit connection between Maxi's bullying and a political stance, and thus connect personal to political domination.

Smith's final alternative to domestic endings involves the entrance of a third character into the divisive world of married couples. In "The Herriots" and in "Sunday at Home," Smith was to experiment with a suggestion, playfully made by Celia in *The Holiday,* that relationships are more bearable with a larger quota of females to males:

I could never marry because of fear, I should like to have one-third of a man, to be the third wife, perhaps, with her own house—einverstanden, it is difficult to share a kitchen—but to be the one wife, that is the dear one and the comfort, to be the dear one, and the comfort of one man, that I admire, that I could not dare to be, I should be afraid there was a lion in the street.[71]

Although the women who enter the lives of the married couples in the two stories are not alternative wives, the presence of these women does serve to lessen the tensions, suggesting that marriage's claustrophobic closeness needs to be opened up with the rhythms of friendship. Threesomes, Smith advises, are always healthier than twosomes.

In "The Herriots," Peg is inextricably bound to closeness with an irresponsible though likable husband, Coke. Their relationship is exemplified by a scene in which the two of them, threatened by poverty, cry miserably together in bed. Yet this claustrophobic isolation opens up through the mysterious entrance of another character, Mrs. Barlow. After her nightmare of a claustrophobic world of families, Peg dreams of a house with the number 101. In true fantasy fashion, her dream ends up the agency of their salvation, since an old widow lives in house number 101 and offers Peg the job of companion. Not only does the job help with their situation of poverty, but the elderly Mrs. Barlow also acts as a needed buffer between Peg and Coke. The story ends with the three of them sitting together, Coke having offered Mrs. Barlow a chocolate bar. We see them as a peaceful threesome, in marked contrast to the earlier scene in which Coke and Peg cried alone.

Another story that ends on a seated threesome is "Sunday at Home," where the claustrophobic quarreling of Glory and her husband, Ivor, is broken up by the entrance of Greta, who brings a brief and somewhat improbable peace back to the couple. Greta first boosts Glory's self-confidence, damaged by Ivor, by claiming that she actually likes Glory's dirty dressing gown and lunch of overcooked meat and undercooked beans. Unlike Ivor, Greta is not judgmental but accepts Glory, which makes a marked change in Glory's mood. Not only does Greta help Glory, but she offers Ivor the attention and affirmation he has been looking for. When Ivor comes in again, Greta is ready to entertain him by looking at his new plastic bait. She pours the cocoa, and the story ends with a cozy domestic setting, represented by a threesome rather than a twosome:

Silence fell upon them in the sun-spiked room. Silently, happily, they went on with their lunch. The only sound now in the room was the faint sizzle of the cocoa against the side of the jug (that was set too close to the fire and soon must crack) and the far off bark of the dog Sultan, happy with his rats.[72]

Although the jug that must soon crack is an ominous hint that this happiness is temporary, Greta's presence, like Mrs. Barlow's, offers a new social patterning, one that approaches Celia's vision of a marriage with three wives. The only problem in this story is that the newly found peace is temporary; there is no way in Smith's world to retain such a peace. However, her brief fantasies offer the comfort and hope that are the purpose of visions.

Through her choice of satire, already a blurred genre, Smith was able to mix savagery with, in the later stories, a kind of comic gentleness. She most likely learned this technique from Humbert Wolfe's monograph on satire, since he argues that satire must be composed of both hate and love.[73] Unable merely to denounce domesticity, Smith was able to use her stories for the purpose of reforming. After all, in her review of Evelyn Waugh's *Scoop*, she claims that satire is a weapon proper to reforming angels, "or at least to the more angelic of our sort; a heart in the right place (and well in hand), a burning indignation, refined to the temper of a steel blade; a reformer's zeal; these are some of its attributes. . . ."[74] Although Smith was to emulate the steel blade of Parker and Loos, she parts company from them in her angelic zeal to transform.

6

The Sung Poems
1957–1971

Stevie Smith's greatest period of fame occurred in the last decade of her life, when she was known for her engaging performances of her poetry. A typical Smith poetry reading included not only the expected recitation of poems, but also the singing of two or three of her works to familiar-sounding tunes. Although Smith often "borrowed" these tunes from Anglican hymns, folk melodies, popular or music hall songs, and an occasional military march, she also created her own tunes, in imitation of the above genres. Dressed in a childlike pinafore and the famous white lace stockings, Smith awed audiences, despite her off-key singing. Oral performances were extremely popular during the period, but Smith was definitely one of the movement's most unexpected stars. Hardly a leather-jacketed "tough," the most common persona of the oral poetry movement, she still drew large crowds with her composite art of poetry and music.

Because Smith's sung poems were a major element of her artistic appeal, one would expect her critics to "read" her performances as well as her printed texts, yet recent criticism on Smith's poetry has been largely silent on the sung poems. For example, poststructuralist Martin Pumphrey sees Smith's playful performances as a purposeful challenge to the seriousness of the literary world; however, his discussion of her poetry focuses only on the printed texts.[1] Even more recent discussions of Smith's poetry have ignored the performance aspect of her work.[2] Smith's biographers have done a thorough job of documenting her performances through reviews and audience reports, but no one has yet examined her sung poems as a boundary-crossing art form, one that provokes a reconsideration of poetic and musical convention.

As with Smith's drawings, beginning a discussion of the sung poems involves opening the Pandora's box of whether her performances were "any good." Even those musicians who are fond of Smith's work often make the comment that she "cannot sing," though sing she did.[3] And at least one group of poets and musicians, in a BBC Third Programme discussion in 1966, declared that her mixing of poetry and singing in the New Moon Carnival rendition of "Do Take Muriel Out" was "extremely simple," "rather primitive," and "not particularly effective."[4] The latter opinion is especially frustrating, since its proponents judge her performance without a discussion of her musical contexts: Smith was hardly vying with operatic sopranos.

Smith's effectiveness, as poet Seamus Heaney attests, was the result of her entire performance, bodily gestures as well as voice. His captivating description of Smith onstage allows us to glimpse the transformation of her poetic texts in performance:

The unknown quantity in my response to the book [*Collected Poems*] was the memory of the poet's own performance of her verse, her voice pitching between querulousness and keening, her quizzical presence at once inviting the audience to yield her their affection and keeping them at bay and a quick irony. She seemed to combine elements of Gretel and of the witch, to be vulnerable and capable, a kind of Home Counties *sean bhean bhoct,* with a hag's wisdom and a girl's wide-eyed curiosity. She chanted her poems artfully off-key, in a beautifully flawed plainsong that suggested two kinds of auditory experience: an embarrassed party-piece by a child half-way between tears and giggles, and a deliberately *faux-naïf* rendition by a virtuoso.[5]

In using her body as a sign, what Heaney calls her "quizzical presence," Smith was already anticipating contemporary feminist performance art, which interrogates and deconstructs cultural definitions of womanhood. As Judith Butler has written of performance, "[P]arodic proliferation deprives hegemonic culture and its critics of the claim to naturalized or essentialist gender identities."[6] As with the old woman in Smith's early story "Surrounded by Children," the mere appearance of her aging body, in this case dressed in child's clothing, defies expectations of the "normal." We do not expect to find an aging woman either in a baby carriage (as in the story) or onstage as a performance artist, often singing what appear to be love songs. Smith's simultaneous appearance as a prepubescent girl and a postmenopausal woman thus shatters traditional notions of womanhood based on sexual attractiveness (the ability to enter into romance) and fertility (the ability to engage in domesticity). In denying the polarities of youth and age, productivity and nonproductivity, Smith's performances acknowledge, as Peggy Phelan has written, that "'the woman' can exist only between . . . categories of analysis."[7]

Smith's "odd" singing no longer seems out of place if we remember that it was accompanied by this "quizzical presence." The records of Heaney and others make it clear that effrontery, not pleasing beauty, was the goal of her performances. Unfortunately, visual records of Smith's performances are limited to these accounts, since her work was preserved only in audiotape. However, both sources together enable us to reconstruct the traditions from which she drew and thereby better understand her goals as a performer. Her combinations of recitation and singing, her use of dramatic characters, and her parodic performances suggest that Smith was highly influenced by the Victorian music hall tradition, a supposition that Smith herself confirms.

Approximately mid-career, Smith became aware of the possibilities of music hall, though her use of that tradition did not begin until late in life. According to Frances Spalding, Smith's interest in performing began in 1944, when she attended a very successful presentation of her work at Homerton, the Cambridge teacher-training college. Five years later, at a performance in which Hedli Anderson sang her poems to Elisabeth Lutyens's settings, many of which were Smith's own tunes, Smith noticed the potential for her poems to act as a mixed media composition in the music hall tradition:

"[T]he audience reacted in a way that made me think perhaps they had better not be looked upon as pure poems but rather as intimate revue stuff, you know, they laughed quite a lot and clapped really like anything. Does this suggest that there might be a wider public for them than the highbrow sort?"[8]

Smith's use of the word *revue,* whose first recorded English usage was in 1872, suggests she is recalling later music hall, since it became identified with variety theater in the 1870s.[9] As in her illustrated poems, Smith was beginning to reject "pure poems," or formalist art, in favor of an art form driven by consideration of its audience and a desire to collapse boundaries between "high" and "low."

Smith's performance history began with her work for the BBC in the forties and, after a break of several years, resumed in the late fifties; however, the BBC's conservative notions of what constituted art constrained rather than developed her performance style. Interestingly, the construction of the BBC during this period prevented Smith's concept of a boundary-crossing art from coming to fruition, at least under its direction. It is her later live recordings, based on many years of performance experience, that show a Stevie Smith involved in redefining poetry, both its generic limitations and its audience appeal. To claim that these tapes are a key to understanding Smith's work is to suggest not that her performance is the only authentic rendition of the work, but instead that her performances give a dimension that has been lost in the duplication of her work by those who understand poetry more traditionally. For example, Glenda Jackson's readings make for painful listening in that they attempt to turn Smith into a serious and solemn poet.[10] Yet Smith's live, festival tapes have never been released and are available only at the National Sound Archive in London. An analysis of Smith's sung poetry is dependent on BBC and British Council tapes, plus a few commercial recordings, and the musical preservation efforts of those who heard her in performance, such as Peter Dickinson, who has provided both a songbook of "Stevie's Tunes" and a tape.[11]

While Stevie Smith was envisioning an art form that would collapse the traditional boundaries between audiences, the BBC was in the process of creating an institutional structure based on clear demarcations between audiences. After World War II, the BBC offered three broadcasts—Third, Home, and Light—programs that roughly corresponded to highbrow, middlebrow, and lowbrow audiences.[12] Though the BBC tried to avoid obvious connections between the Third Programme, which aired almost all poetry presentations, and the cultural elite, these connections were barely suppressed:

The audience addressed was . . . regarded as the already educated and expert. But to avoid charges of elitism Grisewood [an early Third Programme controller] tended to use labels such as "those who care," rather than terms such as "cultivated" or "cultured": "It is for such as these that the Third Programme exists."[13]

Indeed, some contemporary publications recognized that the BBC's hierarchical structure, and particularly its creation of the Third Programme, might act to preserve class distinctions:

Several papers seemed genuinely concerned about the fragmentation of the audience that the advent of the Third Programme might lead to. The *Observer* feared that "it may develop a 'closed shop' in the dissemination of culture"; while the *Daily Worker,* anxious that it might "increase differences of taste and cultural prejudices by dividing the listening public into sheep and goats," saw a solution to the problem in extensive trailing of Third Programme output on the other stations, a practice which the BBC was slow to take up.[14]

Most likely because of this hierarchical structure, which perpetuated traditional notions of "good art," Smith's attempts to sing her poems on radio were rebuffed by BBC producers, thus preventing her unique mixture of poetry and music from being heard until the late 1950s, when she began singing in live performances. Even her readings, many of which were a success, were highly controversial because of what she describes as her "South Kensington accent."[15] If it had not been for the efforts of women such as Anna Kallin and, especially, Rachel Marshall, who was ahead of her time in questioning the BBC's classist pronunciation requirements, Smith might never have been heard on the BBC.[16]

Smith's career at the BBC suggests a general suspicion of her poetry, since she began first as a scriptwriter, then as a performer of her own fiction, and only later as a reader (rather than singer) of poetry. Smith originally wrote two scripts for the BBC, one a program on Thomas Hood, aired March 1946, the other an essay, "Syler's Green," read by Flora Robson, first transmitted on 5 August 1947. Smith then entered her short story "Sunday at Home" in a BBC-sponsored contest, only to have it turned down because the show's producer, D. F. Boyd, found her reading voice "hopeless." Fortunately, Anna Kallin worked with Smith's voice, and Smith was eventually allowed to broadcast the story on 20 March 1949. Smith went on to produce three programs, "Poems and Drawings" (28 March 1951, 18 October 1951, 21 July 1952), based on her poems and their illustrations, as described by Smith. After these, Kallin appears to have lost interest in Smith, and when Smith approached Kallin with the idea of a fourth program, with musical settings for her poems, Kallin put her off. Smith apparently did not intend to sing herself, but the BBC showed no interest in her sung poems.[17]

After a hiatus of four years, Smith was to begin work for the BBC again, this time in a reading of her poems on 12 April 1956, the first of Smith's BBC recordings to have survived. The recording's only interest to a contemporary is the way in which it contrasts with Smith's later recorded performances, such as her triumphant tour-de-force at the Edinburgh Festival in 1965. In this first record of her poetry on the BBC, Smith recites in a traditional, and extremely stiff, manner. After another program, entitled "Too Tired for Words," Smith again attempted to include music in her BBC presentations, this time her own singing. By the end of the fifties, she had begun singing in performance and so it was natural for her to approach the BBC with the idea. However, Douglas Cleverdon, the show's producer, strongly dissuaded Smith from singing. Interestingly, his judgment was based at least partially on gender considerations: "[T]o be tolerable on the air, female singing voices have to be very good indeed." Cleverdon did produce a poetic performance with Smith's tunes, the radio play "A Turn Outside" (broadcast 18 and 23 May 1959), but a woman with a "good" voice, Janette Richer, ended up singing the part in such a way that Smith's irony is entirely stripped from the songs. Smith was so upset, by Richer's performance in particular, that she left the recording session early.[18]

Smith's performance style and sung poetry were therefore to develop in live performances rather than under BBC direction, though her BBC readings may have given her the confidence to venture into this arena. Smith began reading her poetry in 1957, first at the Poetry Society at the Oxford Union on 12 November 1957, and then, eight days later, at a lecture that included sung poems.[19] Many of Smith's subsequent performances addressed poetry's traditional, university-educated audiences, but others moved beyond these. She read three times—1960, 1961, 1962—at the John Lewis department store, a stolid bourgeois haven.[20] Between 1959 and 1968, she performed in at least fifteen of Michael Horovitz's Live New Departure arts circuses, intended to introduce poetry to wider audiences.[21] On 7 December 1968, she did a pub appearance at the Lamb and the Flag, where her large audience nearly collapsed the floor of an upstairs gallery.[22] And then there were her enormously popular festival readings, which fortunately have been preserved on BBC recordings. These recordings in no way resemble her awkward, stiff reading of 1956; in performance she is relaxed and clearly in control of her audience.

That Smith had in mind a different kind of poetic recitation and audience than her BBC producers is clear from her early reference to the tradition of music hall. The most immediate connection between Smith's sung poems and the music hall is that Smith, like many early music hall performers, often relied on the music of others: music hall performers, before the advent of paid composers, often sung their lyrics to borrowed tunes. Most likely, this tradition originated merely to find music for lyrics, since the composition of music requires specialized skills that a performer might not have had. However, borrowing old tunes and giving them new words can also be used to add another layer to a performance.[23] Smith's poems and music, as do her poems and drawings, become two competing texts. Loosely yoked rather than rigorously unified, they require an audience to enact their meaning, one that is available only through the recognition of the cultural "joke." Smith was to use this combination of texts in complicated ways that recall the subversive performances of some of the best-known women music hall artists.

Reading Smith as a subversive performer in the music hall tradition requires an acknowledgment of music hall's complexity as an art form. According to J. S. Bratton, the music hall has been interpreted by "nostalgic apologists" from the music hall itself; "romantic idealists," "who claim the music hall for the folk"; and "the few modern, generally sub-Marxist or cultural-materialist, writers," "who have challenged these interpretations, but offered only reductive accounts and extrinsic models by which to understand a dynamic and complex discourse."[24] Bratton argues for a more complex understanding of music hall, by claiming that performers "do not only reproduce or display ideologies, but contribute to their construction and modification."[25] In this way, Bratton gives credit to some of the performers who worked in what was largely a conservative tradition designed to reproduce ideology. Certainly, as some critics have contended, the music hall's views of love and marriage were often extremely traditional. For instance, Dave Russell claims, "Overall, . . . a woman's place was clearly established. Home, husband, and children were what really mattered."[26] Yet even Russell mentions women performers who refused to conform to expectations, among these Marie Lloyd, Vesta Victoria, and Vesta Tilley.[27] In addition, it must be remembered that Smith was following in the *tradition* of music hall performance, a tradition that has been "remade" into a subversive genre through the "continual selection and re-selection of ancestors," among these Jenny Hill.[28] By relying on this version of the music hall's history, Smith was to maximize the power of her poetry's satiric comments on love and marriage.

Women music hall artists frequently exhibited a multilayered effect through the selection of material that countered tradition and through their bawdy renditions of that material. Artists such as Marie Lloyd are perhaps most often remembered for their satiric mocking of love and marriage. Her choice of "The Cock and Linnet" song countered Victorian notions of domestic ideology, in itself an unspoken text:

> We had to move away
> 'Cos the rent we couldn't pay
> The moving van came round just after dark;
> There was me and my old man
> Shoving things inside the van,
> Which we'd often done before, let me remark.
> . . . .
> My old man said, "Follow the van,
> And don't dilly-dally on the way!"
> Off went the car with the home packed in it,
> I walked behind with my old cock linnet.
> But I dillied and dallied, dallied and dillied,
> Lost the van and don't know where to roam.
> I stopped on the way to have the old half-quartern,
> And I can't find my way to home.[29]

In this song, home is hardly the safe place of middle-class Victorian ideology, as the family must flee their creditors, nor is the wife the perfect domestic ideal, since she is more interested in stopping for a drink than in getting home to her husband. The Victorian home is literally "lost" in the song. In addition, Lloyd's lively rendition of the song served to underline its opposition to unspoken ideology. Lloyd's performances are thus characterized by thickness: the song acting against ideology, the performance adding to the song.

Smith was to add even more in the way of thickness to her performances through references to traditional musical texts, either real texts or imitated ones, rather than Lloyd's more generalized references. Through the doubling up of texts, Smith could add another layer of parody: Her poems thus "send up" these traditional texts, exposing their values as falsely restrictive or overly sentimental. Not all of Smith's sung poems address issues of love and marriage, but many, as has been common among female performers, do take up questions of women's identity vis-à-vis its presentation in popular culture. Others, though they do not specifically address women's concerns, take issue with the hierarchical, and patriarchal, structuring of society. For example, the seemingly nonsensical "Hymn to the Seal," sung to the tune of "Soldiers of Christ Arise," mocks a Christian world that has repeatedly subordinated animals to humans.

Not all Stevie Smith's sung poems are "send-ups," however; like Victorian women music hall artists, Smith possessed a larger repertoire of techniques. Many women music hall artists were known for combining irony with pathos, thus creating texts that not only mocked but also sympathized. For example, Jenny Hill, who was famous for her rapport with female audiences, sang a number about a woman with eleven children, including such lines as "Woe is the woman who owns eleven," "A woman's work is never done," and "Who'd be a mother." In his analysis of Hill, J. S. Bratton notes that one reviewer interpreted the performance as a "straight" presentation of an overburdened woman; on the other hand, another reviewer felt that Hill's facial expressions, used on the chorus line "woe is the mother who owns eleven," were terribly amusing.[30] Apparently, Hill was able to combine pathos for the woman's real counterparts, burdened by excessive childbearing, with mockery at a culture that encourages excessive fertility.

Smith uses dual texts in her sung poems to convey this same combination of irony and pathos. A large number of her sung poems are intoned to what can best be described as "fake plainsong chant," and many of these describe the lives of individual women who have suffered through society's dictates. Smith's poems, or the "top" layer, frequently consist of fairly vicious attacks on these women, duped by feminine dreams, yet the bottom text of plainsong chant serves to give them dignity and sympathy, ennobling the disasters of their lives as tragedies. In addition, Smith could use plainsong chant to underscore the tragedy of rebellious women who lash out at society's dictates, only to be crushed. Her mockery of the impetuousness and naiveté of rebelliousness is countered by the plainsong chant that mourns the loss of these women.

Performance has always been characterized by its ephemerality, but Smith's use of dual texts allows a contemporary reader partially to resurrect her performance, since the direction of its irony and/or sympathy is indicated by her use of another, recoverable text. However, as Henry M. Sayre has suggested, the hallmark of performance art is its undecidability and its reliance on an audience.[31] Any readings of Smith's sung poems are dependent on the angle of the viewer's perception, shaped in my own case by a concern with the history of women artists and theorists who have "retold" their culture, mixing its parts, as does Luce Irigaray, so that they are no longer recoverable in their traditional ordering.

COMIC PARODY

Many of Smith's poems rewrite conventional assumptions through a commandeering of tradition for their own resistant purposes. In this respect, Smith's satiric poems of love and marriage, sung to conventional tunes, can be compared to the IWW's practice of replacing the lyrics of Christian hymns with those of socialist worker songs. Both practices, in the words of Cary Nelson, work to "radically . . . resemanticize" the culture.[32] However, Smith's practice is more complex in that her poems not merely replace the lyrics of the former song, but interrogate the former song's ideology. Smith's "replacement lyrics" therefore imprison the old traditional text, making it work for them.

Smith's practice of writing poems to traditional tunes dates back to her first volume, which includes "To the Tune of the Coventry Carol," her only poem of that volume to be assigned a melody, though the poem does not exist on any surviving recording. Already in the late thirties, before she actually began singing her poems, Smith was envisioning an art form in which her words would resist tradition.

A familiar Christmas carol, "The Coventry Carol" celebrates one of the most sacred and solemn events in the church, the birth of Jesus and the subsequent salvation of his followers. Although a lullaby, actually about King Herod's massacre of the infants, the song participates in the Anglican canon as a part of the celebration of Christmas and the New Year.[33] But in Smith's rendition, the poem ends up questioning society's (and religion's) expectations that all will love and marry, and thus conform, regardless of their individual feelings:

O lovers true
And others too
Whose best is only better
Take my advice
Shun compromise
Forget him and forget her.[34]

Intentionally, Smith gets the point of the carol "wrong," using the carol
for her own resistant purposes, a celebration of love's endings. The poem
finally champions individual freedom and its joys, rather than the sense
of social belonging that is exemplified by a carol, particularly a Christmas
carol.

Another early, unrecorded poem, one that also flouts tradition, although this time secular tradition, is "The Devil-my-Wife," written to
the popular tune of "Golden Slumbers." "Golden Slumbers," like "The
Coventry Carol," is a sweet lullaby; it celebrates either a lover watching
over his beloved or a mother watching over a child:

Golden slumbers kiss your eyes,
Smiles awake you when you rise;
Sleep, pretty darling, do not cry,
And I will sing a lullaby.

Care you know not, therefore sleep,
While I o'er you watch do keep;
Sleep, pretty darling, do not cry,
And I will sing a lullaby.[35]

The song presents home as the traditional place of safety and serenity,
since the loved one promises to "watch" and protect, leaving the beloved
without "care."

Hardly a presentation of home as a serene place, "The Devil-my-
Wife," as might be expected from the title, exposes the sentimentality of
"Golden Slumbers" through the vicious complaints of a husband:

The nervous face of my dear wife
Is covered with a fearful grin,
And nods and becks
Come without checks
As the devils pop out and in.

Gush, then, gush and gabble,
Vanity is your dabble,
And in mediocrity
Is your cruelty.[36]

Figure 6.1. "The Devil-my-Wife"

While relationships are harmonious in "Golden Slumbers," they are discordant and angry in "The Devil-my-Wife." (In Peter Dickinson's arrangement, the song is heavily syncopated and in no way resembles the original waltz tune.)[37] According to the husband, his wife's chatter makes domestic peace impossible. Since his accusations are based on a stereotypical comment about wives—that they talk too much—his denigration of his wife casts doubt on the harmony of not only his marriage, but all marriages. At least from one husband's perspective, peace is impossible to attain in matrimony.

Interestingly, this poem is accompanied by a drawing that adds another layer to this already multilayered composition, though that layer would not be available in performance. In the drawing, the wife is sitting in a chair, reading from a sheaf of papers—a newspaper or a letter, perhaps (fig. 6.1). In silently occupying herself, this wife hardly resembles the "gushing" and "gabbling" wife of the husband's description, and thus casts doubt on the husband's reading of their situation, as well as on the song's traditional message of domesticity. The drawing decenters the original song and the poem itself; both end up cast as traditionalist texts that cannot necessarily be trusted. Marriage as bliss and marriage as eternal sex war are similarly called into question by the poet.

Songs in which Smith parodies a text, either an actual text or an imitated one, fortunately exist on recordings. One poem set to a traditional tune that Smith performed frequently is "The Warden," which shows up on both the Marvel Press recording, Smith's main commercial recording, and on a BBC television feature, though only a sound track is now available.[38] On the Marvel LP, the song is sandwiched between readings of two poems, "If I lie down" and "'Oh stubborn race of Cadmus' seed . . . ,'" both of which narrate stories of rebellious individuals; "The Warden," a poem about a man's stifling love, thus acts as a reminder of the ways in which tradition may bind, despite the desire to escape. In the television appearance, "The Warden" appears after another "send-up" of domestic ideology, "I Remember," which jokingly tells of a disastrous wedding night. "I Remember" can also be related to the music hall in that it falls into a common music hall genre, one that was also subversive of Victorian domestic ideology: the tale of the wedding night that goes wrong.[39] "The Warden" therefore continues the spirit of "I Remember," preparing for the escapist poem that follows, "Look!" In alternating poems that mock tradition with poems that encourage escape and resistance, Smith developed a performance mode that called for the revisioning of tradition, as well as its destruction.

In performance, "The Warden" is sung, as was the intention for "The Devil-my-Wife," to a sweet, melodious song, here a Victorian parlor song entitled "The Children's Home." The first line of the song, "They played in their beautiful gardens," is incorrectly noted by Smith as "They played in the beautiful garden." The original song's thematic focus, as with "Golden Slumbers," is the innocence and sweetness of love, in this instance between a wealthy boy and a "beggar maiden":

> Once he had given her a flow'r!
> And oh! how he smiled to see
> Her thin white hands thro' the railings
> Stretched out so eagerly.[40]

The two poems can be further compared in that the "top" layer of the composite art form, the poems themselves, reveal the dissonant and cruel side of heterosexual relationships, against a background of harmonious music.

Although presumably a poem about a young girl who is spirited away by the fairies, "The Warden" can also be read as the narrative of a jealous lover whose desire to possess his beloved ends up in her demise:

> The Warden has decked her with seaweed,
> And shells of an ancient design,
> But she sighs as she presses his fingers,
> My heart can never be thine.[41]

128

"The Warden" is not only a fairy spirit but a cruel lover or husband who objectifies his beloved, decorating her with clothes (seaweed) and jewels (shells of an ancient design), finally treating her as a child who must not wander from his sight.

The child-wife eventually expires from an inability to pursue her own life, though her expiration would seem to be a living death, since she turns into a "sea-green stone," an image that recalls woman's traditional entombment in silence and lack of expression:

> He sits in the golden chair
> With the child he would call his own,
> But the beautiful child has expired,
> He nurses a sea-green stone.

As in "The Devil-my-Wife," marriage is seen as an unyielding trap, one in which a wife's identity is slowly subsumed by the prevalent cultural identity, as mindless gossip in the former poem, or as gorgeous object in "The Warden." Having been decked with jewels, she becomes a jewel herself, the sea-green stone.

The above poems rely on actual tunes, but Smith would often create her own tunes in imitation of traditional genres. Like the previous texts, these often ironically refer to an "under" text. One of these is "Silence and Tears," recorded on the Marvel LP, though no doubt sung in performance as well.[42] "Silence and Tears," which narrates the story of a dead man's burial and the response of his family, is sung to an upbeat military march: The tune befits a military man, though it does not fit this occasion, his death. Smith uses the upbeat tune to underline his family's relief at his death, and thus the disparity between tune and poem reveals a disparity between emotions and expectations. In printed form, the poem is juxtaposed with a conventional drawing in which family and friends gather round an open grave, the wife and children's heads bowed in what appears to be sorrow (fig. 6.2). However, the poem reveals a family that is anything but sorrowful.

The lack of fit between the tune and the occasion is emphasized by lines that must be rushed in order to fit the tune, thereby underlining the haste with which this supposedly respectable husband and father is being disposed of. The first stanza fits nicely in the tune, but the second stanza does not: "took the tears and the rain" ends up compacted into a musical line that is not long enough.[43] The lack of fit between song and poem, the poem "lapping" over the song, gives a comic feel to what should be a tragic poem.

Although it concerns religion's hypocrisy in dealing with death, the

Figure 6.2. "Silence and Tears"

poem ends by focusing on the military man's family, and thus becomes a comment on marriage and domesticity:

> And may the coffin hold his bones in peace that lies below,
> And may the widow woman's tears make a good show,
> And may the suitable priestly garment not let the breath of
>   scandal through.
>
> For the weather of their happening has been a little inclement,
> And would people be so sympathetic if they knew how the
>   story went?
> Best not put it to the test. Silence and tears are convenient.

The widow appears to be crying at the beginning of the poem, but by the end of the poem we find out that her tears are false: "may the widow woman's tears make a good show." The widow's inability to cry is explained by Smith as the result of a breakdown in family unity, caused, or causing, a scandal. The line "the weather of their happening has been a little inclement" is absurdly funny in its understatement, and made funnier by the fact that the rhymes of the last stanza are off: inclement, went, convenient (unlike the rhymes of the previous stanzas, such as man, ran, began). The word *inclement* does not fit the poem, rhythmically speaking, and apparently hardly begins to describe the problems between the military man and his widow. As contemporary poet Tina Darragh points out, Smith is often at her most subversive in her rhymes, their "offness" frequently indicating behaviors that do not conform to society's directives.[44]

Smith's vagueness about the family's tragedy leads to continued questioning of domestic ideology's promises, since the audience must come up with their own increasingly dire scenarios for what has happened. Smith cleverly encourages her listeners to consider all the various ways by which a marriage might end tragically, and thus all the reasons that love and marriage are a precarious undertaking. Is the scandal referred to in the poem merely a story of a contentious husband and wife, bored with each other's company? Or has there been infidelity? Or possibly the tale's narrator is hinting at something worse—perhaps she has killed her husband or participated in his death? The vagueness of the poem reveals that conventions of the grieving family leave no room for other truths, some of which may be truly horrible. Social sentiments of love are seen to be a sham, hiding other, more ugly truths.

A second example of a poem sung to one of Smith's own tunes, and one that similarly undoes domestic ideology, is "Le Désert de l'Amour," recorded by the British Council on 31 December 1968.[45] The song begins as a sweet-sounding love tune but quickly turns into a mournful chant, revealing how Smith could mix genres in her sung poems. The poem therefore comments on both the joys of love, as reflected in popular songs, and the solemnity and sacredness of love, as established by church traditions.

The first stanza acts as an imitation love song in which the lover claims his devotion:

> I want to be your pinkie
> I am tender to you
> My heart opens like a cactus flower
> Do you thinky I will do?[46]

However, even in this sweet stanza, signs of potential dissension between lover and beloved exist, since the flower that signifies his heart is a "cactus flower," flower of aridity, rather than the traditional flower of love, the rose. In addition, the last line of the stanza, "Do you thinky I will do," needs another syllable—the *y* on *thinky*—to fit the musical pattern of the love song, and therefore begins to suggest to an audience or reader that love songs are constraining and ill fitting, at least in these lovers' experience.

The second stanza moves even farther away from a love song in parodying or satirically repeating the first stanza—the heart is a cactus, not a cactus flower—and thus exposes the poem's antiromantic intentions. The couple's love is clearly doomed, as is any idealistic, romantic love:

> My heart is like a cactus
> Not like a cactus flower
> And I can kill love
> Without entering her bower.

Although the song is still sung to the same sweet tune, Smith parodies it further, allowing her audience to feel the reality of love between this couple slipping farther and farther away from the social ideal, perfect rhapsodic intimacy.

The last stanza falls completely out of its love song tune and into plainsong chant, a transition that both underscores the tragedy of the collapsing relationship and underlines the way in which the relationship falls short of religious and romantic ideals. The distance between ideology and actual emotion is again made clear by the lack of fit between words and music. Whereas there were formerly too few words for the music, there are now too many, the last lines sounding literally forced into their solemn tune. The eeriness of this tune, after the bright love song, suggests that something darker than the mere loss of love has occurred:

> So they both thought. But he was silent and she said:
> I cannot see which way you are pointing, the sky is so dark red,
> And when the sandstorm is over I shall lie down on my bed.

Has the husband purposefully lost his wife in the sandstorm, and contributed to her death? This threat or suggestion of violence hovers just beneath the surface, hinting at the basic instability of heterosexual relationships as they have been traditionally configured.

All of the five poems discussed above can be read, without their music, as revealing Smith's distrust and suspicion of love and marriage. However, when paired with music, these poems become something more, commentaries on the way in which ideology binds. Smith's speakers try to crowd the "content" of their lives into society's forms, represented by Smith's tunes, but the poems woefully tell of the lack of fit. Domestic ideology gives these characters no way to tell the stories of their lives, whether they be scandals or mere unhappiness or even violence. As in Smith's other poems, it is women who suffer the most in trying to pour their lives into society's molds, since they are faced with either the usurpation of their identities or the loss of life itself.

PARODY AND PATHOS

Although Smith used her sung poems to ridicule conventions of love and marriage, she also relied on the musical element of her performances to provide pathos, both for women duped by dreams of domestic ideology and for those whose rebellions against domestic ideology end in tragedy. When the central focus of her sung poem is a single woman's narrative, Smith often makes use of what Heaney called "beautifully flawed plainsong" to ennoble her fallen women. Drawing from Christianity's tradition of turning its victims into martyrs, Smith imitated church music in order to create a new kind of martyr, the woman who cannot succeed according to society's dictates. Her sung poems thus rewrite the traditions of Christianity for her own resistant purposes.

One of the poems in which Smith used plainsong to add pathos is "The Repentance of Lady T," sung at Smith's famous appearance in Edinburgh on 27 August 1965.[47] The poem (and its accompanying drawing) are particularly satiric and perhaps even cruel, as Lady T's plight is largely mocked. The title of the poem, "The Repentance of Lady T," would seem to indicate a major religious conversion in the life of a woman who has committed egregious sins.[48] However, the poem narrates no such story. Like T. S. Eliot's "The Love Song of J. Alfred Prufrock," the title in its weightiness serves only to diminish an already diminished character. Lady T's "sins" are few in number, consisting mainly of vanity and a lack of direction, if the latter can be called a sin. The accompanying drawing shows Lady T in front of her mirror, combing her already curled hair. She is dressed fairly elaborately for Smith's drawings, in a frilled petticoat and stockings (fig. 6.3).

For a brief moment, Lady T is a sympathetic character, a woman who has accidentally lost herself in trying to be the woman, all surface and no substance, whom she sees in the mirror.

Figure 6.3. "The Repentance of Lady T"

> I look in the glass
> Whose face do I see?
> It is the face
> Of Lady T.

However, Lady T quickly loses our sympathy in the second stanza as her distress turns to a whine, revealing her lack of commitment toward change as well as her passivity. She calls upon the Lamb of God to *change her,* leaving all spiritual soul-searching up to the Almighty:

> I wish to change,
> How can that be?
> Oh Lamb of God
> Change me, change me.

Brief and hardly serious, Lady T's "repentance" ends almost as soon as it begins. On the printed page, Lady T hardly receives sympathy.

And yet the plainsong chant to which Smith sings Lady T's lament ennobles her pitiful and rather unremarkable life. Passivity, the chant would seem to indicate, is part of the definition of womanhood, just as is preoccupation with appearance. Detaching oneself from the sung poem of

Lady T in order to condemn or satirize her vanity is harder than detaching oneself from the printed version, since the chant adds sympathy and understanding to her plight.

Another sung poem that works in much the same way is "Do Take Muriel Out," sung at both the Edinburgh Festival and the New Moon Carnival.[49] This poem attracts interest not only because of its appearance in these two major performances, but also because it was the subject of a 1966 BBC discussion, the only one of Smith's sung poems to have received a critique of any sort.

The young woman in "Do Take Muriel Out" is as directionless as Lady T, although in much worse psychological condition, as the poem relates her psychic disintegration and eventual death. Much to her detriment, Muriel, like Lady T, has conformed without questioning society's expectations. That Muriel is looking for a suitor to save her is indicated by the poem's refrain, "Do Take Muriel Out," "out" indicating, at least in the beginning of the poem, a date.[50]

But Muriel is anything but successful, her searches for a mate leading her literally nowhere, to the dysphoric ending of the romance plot, death. At the end of the poem, Death, personified as a gentleman caller, comes to take Muriel "out," this time meaning out of life. Despite Muriel's death, she is too nebulous a character to create much sympathy. Indeed, in her "Poems and Drawings" series, Smith's introduction makes it clear that we are not to side with Muriel's search for rich friends and ultimately a rich husband:

The poems often make use of stories and legends to show what happens when people get lost or go astray in their thoughts and so do not get home. Here is a poem about Muriel; she is standing in her petticoat looking sorrowfully into a mirror, she holds in her hand a large theatrical crown. Muriel looked for her lost friends in the Palace among the rich people, but they were not there.[51]

In this early rendition of Muriel, Smith uses her as a character in a morality play.

It is Smith's sung version that yields Muriel sympathy, as the plainsong gives Smith's poem a mournful sadness. However, as several critics noticed, Smith's performance of "Do Take Muriel Out" at the New Moon Carnival received laughter rather than tears, and her critics, poets and musicians, concluded that Smith's version was a failure.[52] What they did not take into account is their own admission that the audience's laughter was nervous in character. It is funny, after all, that Muriel is expecting a suitor but ends up with Death, who dances her "over the blasted heath" rather than across a ballroom. The laughter underlines the melodramatic nature of Muriel's life, and society's views of women, since the lack of a date ends in death. Also, as in Smith's drawings, the romance plot's euphoric ending becomes entangled with the dysphoric, as Death at the door is characterized as a particularly bad blind date. But the nervousness of the laughter indicates the audience's inability to laugh wholeheartedly at Muriel's plight; the situation is funny, but Muriel herself, who has cried and prayed, is not. The audience's response reveals the "thickness" of the sung version: one layer mocks the dysphoric ending of the romance plot, while another mourns those who are isolated by society's conventions.

"The Heavenly City," though unrecorded, refers to a specific church song, in this case, "Jerusalem the Golden." The solemnness of the hymn underscores the loneliness of the speaker:

> I sigh for the heavenly country,
> Where the heavenly people pass.[53]

Like Muriel, this woman is an outsider who can find no sense of belonging, yet she also receives Smith's pity. Through Smith's use of "Jerusalem the Golden," she becomes not merely a lonely woman, but one of the martyrs mentioned in the song's lyrics.

This sung text exhibits a thickness not available in the previous two texts, since the hymn also works to build the speaker "another world," outside tangible reality. Here, the music, as is possible with Smith's drawings, creates another place or space. In the hymn, Jerusalem is a place of beauty that surpasses earth:

> Oh, land that see'st no sorrow! Oh, state that
>   fear'st no strife!
> Oh, royal land of flowers! Oh, realm and
>   home of life![54]

By means of this ur-text, the spinster is encouraged to dream of her own way out:

> I walk in the heavenly field,
> With lilies and poppies bright,
> I am dressed in a heavenly coat
> Of polished white.

After all, heaven represents the ultimate Utopia, and Smith uses it here to create a place in which the text's speaker is not merely a lonely spinster, a martyr, but a denizen of a brave new world.

Other of Smith's sung poems champion not only the downtrodden, but also the rebellious who fall. For example, "'Oh stubborn race Of Cadmus' Seed . . .'" sung on the Marvel LP to plainsong chant, retells the story of Antigone.[55] Smith's Antigone, as is made clear by the drawing that accompanies the poem and her comments on the poem in her "Poems and Drawings" broadcast, is a naive innocent who does not know what she is up against: "Antigone in this poem is a very young girl, she stands with bows in her hair."[56] Like Lady T and Muriel, she is caught in a world whose rules are not of her making. She rebels, unlike them, but her rebellion ends merely in her own death: In the poem, she walks in the Dark Hall of Hades. Antigone, Smith suggests by depicting her as a girl, is not wise in thinking that her defiance will result in a change of order.

Yet Smith's chant also raises her to a martyr, more courageous than the speaker of "The Heavenly City," a woman whom Smith calls, in her introduction to the poem in the "Poems and Drawings" broadcast, a "true pilgrim":

With conscious godliness she has risen to an occasion but she is going to make sure that the dread judges of hell, Rhadamanthus and Hades, understand quite plainly that she has been put on. And moreover that she forgives her sister. To forgive that feeble little beast, Ismene, that is something, eh? This conviction of divine interest in the face of Death and Indifference is quite splendid, it is the mark of a true pilgrim.[57]

Thus, Smith uses music both to mourn Antigone's loss, and to champion her resistance.

Smith's pathos for women's constraints was to extend even to herself, a woman poet in an inhospitable time period, through her poem "One of Many," recorded at the Edinburgh Festival.[58] While "One of Many" presumably refers to a young child who is killed for rebelling against his elders, Smith was frequently to identify herself, as a poet, with this child:

> Murder in the first degree, cried Old Fury,
> Recording the verdict of the jury.
>
> Now they are come to the execution tree.
> The gallows stand wide. Ah me, ah me.
>
> Christ died for sinners, intoned the Prison
>   Chaplain from his miscellany.
> Weeping bitterly the little child cries: I die
>   one of many.[59]

When the poem is read with Smith as the little child, it mourns Smith's metaphoric death at the hands of an establishment of literary judges. Like the rebellious Antigone, she is made to suffer death, this time emotional death, at the hands of the patriarchs. Her lilting plainsong acknowledges and simultaneously mocks the rule of the patriarchs, since after all she is not the young child in the poem, the one who dies, but the poem's author, who survives to write.

Unlike Victorian music hall artists Jenny Hill and Marie Lloyd, Smith did not sing her poems in an era noted for its repression, which perhaps accounts for her fairly uniform popularity and acceptance. And yet Smith's late fame should be read not merely as a result of changing attitudes toward women's roles, but as part of that process of change. When Smith sang at festivals, she was often the only woman poet scheduled to appear, an elderly woman in a pale pink shift amongst a group of leather-jacketed young men. Perhaps the best example of this incongruity is her infamous appearance with the "poet toughs" in Brussels; while they got drunk and passed out onstage, she quelled the crowd and gave her performance.[60] Her presence amongst the toughs was both a woman's triumph and a reminder that the poetry world was still largely a masculine one.

Smith's antidomestic performance texts need to be read not only as a reflection of changing attitudes, but, in their small way, as a contribution to those attitudes. Bratton's description of the resistant potential of music hall performances also applies to Smith's work: "[P]erformances do not only reproduce or display ideologies, but contribute to their construction and modification."[61] As in an allied art form, musical comedy, her combination of narrative and song encouraged a dual relation with the audience, a duality that Thomas Leitch has described as "identification with the characters, which seeks to erase the differences, and identification with the apparatus, which seeks to maintain them."[62] Smith's combination was particularly radical in that narrative and song occurred simultaneously, without allowing her audience to lapse into passive identification with story.

In encouraging her audiences to simultaneously sympathize and mock, Smith honored women's historic restrictions while at the same time undoing them. Although Smith was never affiliated with a feminist movement, her life fitting almost perfectly into the trough between Edwardian feminism and the women's liberation movement, her antidomestic emphasis resembles that of a more famous writer of the sixties, Betty Friedan. Smith owned a copy of *The Feminine Mystique,* though she never reviewed it and we will never know what she thought of it.[63] Possibly, she would have been bored, since she had been writing her own version for the past thirty years, and across many genres and media.

138

Notes

Index

Notes

CHAPTER 1. INTRODUCTION

1. Two biographies have been published on Smith: Jack Barbera and William McBrien, *Stevie: A Biography of Stevie Smith* (New York: Oxford UP, 1987), and Frances Spalding, *Stevie Smith: A Critical Biography* (London: Faber and Faber, 1988). Barbera, McBrien, and Helen Bajan's bibliography, *Stevie Smith: A Bibliography* (Westport, Conn.: Meckler, 1987) lists a section of published interviews, two of which are reprinted in the Sanford Sternlicht anthology *In Search of Stevie Smith* (Syracuse, N.Y.: Syracuse UP, 1991). Kay Dick's *Ivy and Stevie* (London: Duckworth, 1971, 1983) contains a reminiscence, while, as Romana Huk points out, Sanford Sternlicht's *Stevie Smith* presents largely a biographical reading (Boston: Twayne, 1990).

2. Romana Huk, "Eccentric Concentrism: Traditional Poetic Forms and Refracted Discourse in Stevie Smith's Poetry," *Contemporary Literature* 34.2 (1993): 243.

3. Huk 242.

4. Alison Light, "Outside History? Stevie Smith, Women Poets and the National Voice," *English* 43.177 (Autumn 1994): 240.

5. Barbera and McBrien 41–42.

6. See Deirdre Beddoe, *Back to Home and Duty: Women between the Wars, 1918–1939* (London: Pandora, 1989), and Martin Pugh, *Women and the Women's Movement in Britain, 1914–1959* (London: Macmillan, 1992).

7. Rachel Blau DuPlessis, *Writing beyond the Ending: Narrative Strategies of Twentieth-Century Women Writers* (Bloomington: Indiana UP, 1985), 3.

8. Huk 242.

9. Barbera and McBrien 105 (Narcissa Crowe-Wood); Spalding 102–3 (Narcissa Crowe-Wood), 170–71 (Kay Dick), and 174 (Norah Smallwood).

10. Although the Barbera-McBrien biography is in many ways the better of the two biographies, Spalding's biography is much stronger on Smith's friendships with women.

11. Stevie Smith's letters are located in the Naomi Mitchison Papers at the National Library of Scotland, Edinburgh.

12. Andreas Huyssen, "Mass Culture as Woman: Modernism's Other," *After the Great Divide* (Bloomington: Indiana UP, 1986), 46.

13. Martin Pumphrey, "Play, Fantasy, and Strange Laughter: Stevie Smith's Uncomfortable Poetry," in Sternlicht, *In Search of Stevie Smith* 101.

14. Beddoe 137.

15. Beddoe 136.

16. Beddoe 139.

17. Stevie Smith, *Over the Frontier* (New York: Pinnacle Books, 1982), 153.

18. Stevie Smith, "Family Affair," *Books of the Month* 72.3 (March 1957): 9.

19. Stevie Smith, *The Holiday* (New York: Pinnacle Books, 1982), 160–63.

20. Pumphrey 101.

21. Stevie Smith, "The Better Half?" *Me Again: Uncollected Writings of Stevie Smith,* ed. Jack Barbera and William McBrien (New York: Vintage, 1983), 178.

22. Stevie Smith, "Poems in Petticoats," *Me Again* 181.

23. Julia Kristeva, "Women's Time," *The Kristeva Reader,* ed. Toril Moi (New York: Columbia UP, 1986), 194.

24. Kristeva 209.

25. Pugh 209.

26. Beddoe 3.

27. Beddoe 4.

28. Pugh 209.

29. Barbera and McBrien 41–42, 100.

30. Pugh 210.

31. Rosita Forbes, "Toys and Love," illustrated by Balliol Salmon, *The Royal Magazine,* January 1923, 230.

32. Forbes 232.

33. Forbes 236.

34. Christine Whiting Parmenter, "Lynette the Plain One," illustrated by Pern Bird, *Pearson's Magazine,* January 1923, 49–58.

35. Esther Kent, "Was Her Husband False?" *Peg's Paper,* 2 January 1923, 6.

36. Kent 7.

37. K. U. Green, "Her Sister's Sweetheart," *Peg's Paper,* 2 January 1923, 18–22, 31; Kathleen O'Halloran, "A Girl Should Never Tell," *Peg's Paper,* 2 January 1923, 23–26.

38. Parmenter 54.

39. Forbes 229, 232.

40. Green 19.

41. Philippa King, "The Man Who Came Between," *Peg's Paper,* 7 January 1930, 1–18.

42. Dorothy Marshall, "Was It a Sin?" *Peg's Paper,* 5 January 1935, 3.

43. Mary Roberts Rhinehart, "Her Night of Triumph," *Pearson's Magazine,* January 1923, 95.

44. Fanny Heaslip Lea, "Rosaleen Says Yes," *The Royal Magazine,* January 1923, 305–16.

45. Dorothy Ward, "When I Fell in Love," *Peg's Companion,* 2 January 1923, 14.

46. Peg's Man Pal, "The Too-Independent Girl," *Peg's Paper,* 2 January 1923, 26.

47. Peg's Man Pal 26.

48. Billie Melman, *Women and the Popular Imagination in the Twenties* (New York: St. Martin's Press, 1988), 150.

49. Shari Benstock, *Textualizing the Feminine: On the Limits of Genre* (Norman: U of Oklahoma P, 1991), 142.

50. Stevie Smith, *Novel on Yellow Paper* (New York: Pinnacle Books, 1982), 168.

51. Smith, *Novel* 169.

52. Smith, *Novel* 170–71.

53. Smith, *Novel* 171.

54. Smith, *Novel* 172.

55. Smith, *Novel* 169–70.

56. Smith, *Novel* 169.

57. Mica Nava, *Changing Cultures: Feminism, Youth, and Consumerism* (London: Sage Publications, 1992), 166.

58. See Pugh; Dolores Hayden, *Redesigning the American Dream: The Future of Housing, Work, and Family Life* (New York: Norton, 1984); and Sheila Jeffreys, *The Spinster and Her Enemies: Feminism and Sexuality, 1880–1930* (London: Pandora, 1985).

59. Smith, *Novel* 80.

60. Rachel Bowlby, *Just Looking: Consumer Culture in Dreiser, Gissing, and Zola* (New York: Methuen, 1985), 20, and Nava 185.

61. Rita Felski, *The Gender of Modernity* (Cambridge: Harvard UP, 1995), 63.

62. Kate Flint, *The Woman Reader: 1837–1914* (Oxford: Clarendon Press, 1993), 4, 53–60, 73.

63. Janice A. Radway, *Reading the Romance: Women, Patriarchy, and Popular Literature* (Chapel Hill: U of North Carolina P, 1984, 1991), 211, 222.

64. Angela McRobbie, "Dance and Social Fantasy," in *Gender and Generation,* ed. Angela McRobbie and Mica Nava (London: Macmillan, 1984), 159–60.

65. Thomas Leitch, "Passivity Squared Equals Activism: An Alternative to the Myth of the Inscribed Audience," in *Styles of Cultural Activism,* ed. Philip Goldstein (Newark: U of Delaware P, 1994), 99.

66. Leitch 99.

67. Smith, *Holiday* 142.

68. Stevie Smith, "History or Poetic Drama?" *Me Again* 152.

69. Flint 76–79, 151.

70. Mikhail Bakhtin, "Discourse in the Novel," *The Dialogic Imagination,* ed. Michael Holquist (Austin: U of Texas P, 1981), 288.

71. Bakhtin, "Discourse" 272.

72. Mikhail Bakhtin, *Rabelais and His World,* trans. Helene Iswolsky (Cambridge: M.I.T. Press, 1968), 5.

73. Luce Irigaray, *Speculum of the Other Woman,* trans. Gillian C. Gill (Ithaca, N.Y.: Cornell UP, 1985), 142.

74. Toril Moi, *Sexual/Textual Politics* (New York: Methuen, 1985), 140.

75. Gail M. Schwab, "Irigarayan Dialogism: Play and Powerplay," in *Feminism, Bakhtin, and the Dialogic,* ed. Dale M. Bauer and S. Jaret McKinstry (Albany: State U of New York P, 1991), 61.

76. Griselda Pollock, *Vision and Difference: Femininity, Feminism, and the Histories of Art* (London and New York: Routledge, 1988), 164–65.

77. Stephen Heath, "Lessons from Brecht," *Screen* 15.2 (1974): 104.

78. Linda Hutcheon, *The Poetics of Postmodernism: History, Theory, Fiction* (New York and London: Routledge, 1988), 88, 218–21; see also Ellen E. Berry's *Curved Thought and Textual Wandering* (Ann Arbor: U of Michigan P, 1992) and Pamela L. Caughie's *Virginia Woolf and Postmodernism: Literature in Quest and Question of Itself* (Urbana: U of Illinois P, 1991).

79. Linda Hutcheon, *The Politics of Postmodernism* (London and New York: Routledge, 1989) 119.

80. Pumphrey 97–113.

81. Hutcheon, *Poetics* 220.

82. Hutcheon, *Poetics* 6–7.

83. Judith Butler, *Bodies That Matter: On the Discursive Limits of "Sex"* (New York and London: Routledge, 1993), 10.

84. Michael Gardiner, *The Dialogics of Critique* (London and New York: Routledge, 1992), 171–72, 182.

85. Alison Light, *Forever England: Femininity, Literature, and Conservatism between the Wars* (London: Routledge, 1991), 10.

86. Light, "Outside History?" 250–52.

87. Stevie Smith, "My Muse," *Me Again* 126.

CHAPTER 2. THE NOVELS: 1936–1949

1. Jack Barbera and William McBrien, *Stevie: A Biography of Stevie Smith* (New York: Oxford UP, 1987), 85–99 (*Novel on Yellow Paper*), 111–16 (*Over the Frontier*), and 172–73 (*The Holiday*).

2. Kathleen Wheeler, *"Modernist" Women Writers and Narrative Art* (New York: New York UP, 1994), 142.

3. Elaine Showalter, *A Literature of Their Own: British Women Novelists from Bronte to Lessing* (Princeton: Princeton UP, 1977), 298.

4. Ellen G. Friedman and Miriam Fuchs, "Contexts and Continuities: An Introduction to Women's Experimental Fiction in English," in *Breaking the Sequence: Women's Experimental Fiction,* ed. Ellen G. Friedman and Miriam Fuchs (Princeton: Princeton UP, 1989), 5.

5. Barbera and McBrien 85 (Stein), 87–88 (Sterne), and 88 (Loos).

6. Barbera and McBrien 45, 97–98.

7. Wheeler 142.

8. See Dorothy M. Richardson, Foreword, *Pilgrimage,* 3 vols. (New York: Knopf, 1967), 1:9–12, and Virginia Woolf, *A Room of One's Own* (New York: Harcourt Brace Jovanovich, 1929), 93–98. Barbera and McBrien, who link Smith to her Victorian ancestors, do not comment on any irony in Smith's admiration for the Victorians (168). However, it is important to note that Smith often critiques

the Victorians while purporting to admire them. Her discussion of the workings of Providence in *Mrs. Halliburton's Troubles* and *Lost Sir Massingberd* is a case in point. See also her "retelling" of Tennyson's *Maud* in "Over-Dew," her short story incorporated into *The Holiday* (New York: Pinnacle Books, 1982), 159–63.

9. Stevie Smith, *Novel on Yellow Paper*, preface by Mary Gordon, introduction by Janet Watts (New York: Pinnacle Books, 1982), 14.

10. Smith, *Novel* 14.

11. James Payn, *Lost Sir Massingberd* (New York: Arno Press, 1976); Mrs. Humphry Ward, *Mrs. Halliburton's Troubles* (London: Richard Bentley and Son, 1890.

12. Smith, *Novel* 15.

13. Smith, *Novel* 14.

14. Smith, *Novel* 14.

15. Smith, *Novel* 14.

16. Smith, *Novel* 14.

17. Payn 18.

18. Smith, *Novel* 9.

19. Virginia Woolf, *Three Guineas* (San Diego: Harcourt Brace Jovanovich, 1966), 51.

20. Joyce Carol Oates, "A Child with a Cold, Cold Eye," *New York Times Book Review*, 3 October 1982, 11.

21. Rachel Blau DuPlessis, *Writing beyond the Ending: Narrative Strategies of Twentieth-Century Women Writers* (Bloomington: Indiana UP, 1985), 47–48, 142–43.

22. Alison Light, *Forever England: Femininity, Literature, and Conservatism between the Wars* (London: Routledge, 1991), 160.

23. Mary Poovey, "Feminism and Deconstruction," *Feminist Studies* 14.1 (Spring 1988): 52–53.

24. Smith, *Novel* 14, 93.

25. Barbera and McBrien (96) note the connection between *Yellow* and Pearson publications.

26. Smith, *Novel* 21.

27. Ann Ardis, *New Women, New Novels: Feminism and Early Modernism* (New Brunswick, N.J.: Rutgers UP, 1990), 39.

28. As Ardis has argued, the "New Woman novel needs to be factored into our genealogies of high modernism" (169).

29. Wheeler 149–50; Smith, *Novel* 182.

30. See Julia Kristeva's discussion of the woman writer in *About Chinese Women, The Kristeva Reader*, ed. Toril Moi (New York: Columbia UP, 1986), 155–58, esp. 156.

31. Kate Flint, *The Woman Reader: 1837–1914* (Oxford: Clarendon Press, 1993), 94.

32. Jane Marcus, "Thinking Back through Our Mothers," in *New Feminist Essays on Virginia Woolf* (Lincoln: U of Nebraska P, 1981), 3. Flint (257–59) also comments on the power that women derive through quotation.

33. See, for example, Irigaray's quotation from Freud's "Femininity" that

opens *Speculum*. The quoted passage begins with Freud mulling over the nature of femininity, but cuts off after he dismisses women from the discussion: "to those who are women this will not apply—you are yourselves the problem." The absurdity of this statement is made manifest by Irigaray's decision to end the quotation after this sentence. Luce Irigaray, *Speculum*, trans. Gillian C. Gill (Ithaca, N.Y.: Cornell UP, 1985), 13.

34. Smith, *Novel* 52.

35. Smith, *Novel* 51–52; *sic* is Smith's, denoting a mistake in the church bulletin she is quoting.

36. Smith, *Novel* 242.

37. Rosalind Coward, *Female Desires: How They Are Sought, Bought, and Packaged* (New York: Grove Press, 1985), 13–14.

38. Smith, *Novel* 97.

39. Wheeler 159.

40. Wheeler 157.

41. Smith, *Novel* 146–47. Compare with Euripides, *The Bacchae*, translated by Donald Sutherland (Lincoln: U of Nebraska P, 1968), 4.

42. Smith, *Novel* 151. Compare with Euripides 57–70.

43. Barbera and McBrien 36.

44. Smith, *Novel* 168.

45. Lyof Tolstoi, *The Live Corpse, The Dramatic Works of Lyof N. Tolstoi*, trans. Nathan Haskell Dole (New York: Thomas Y. Crowell, 1923), 253–326.

46. Smith, *Novel* 265–66.

47. Smith, *Novel* 267.

48. Marie Scott-James, "News from Nowhere," *London Mercury* 37 (February 1938): 456.

49. Oates 26.

50. Victoria Glendinning, "Sturm in a Teacup," *Times Literary Supplement*, 18 Jan. 1980, 54.

51. Barbera and McBrien 112.

52. DuPlessis 15. As Rachel DuPlessis has shown, the romance plot punishes a heroine for failing to incorporate herself into society by expelling her, often through death.

53. Elaine Showalter, *The Female Malady: Women, Madness, and English Culture, 1830–1980* (New York: Penguin, 1985), 134.

54. Stevie Smith, *Over the Frontier* (New York: Pinnacle Books, 1982), 79.

55. Smith, *Frontier* 18.

56. Smith, *Frontier* 26.

57. Smith, *Frontier* 81.

58. Showalter, *Female Malady* 138.

59. Smith, *Frontier* 116.

60. Showalter, *Female Malady* 139.

61. Woolf, *Three Guineas* 21.

62. Smith, *Frontier* 228.

63. Smith, *Frontier* 247.

64. Smith, *Frontier* 248.

65. Paul Fussell discusses the "gross dichotomizing" that occurred as the result of World War I, yet he does not make the connection between this trait and masculine gender. See Paul Fussell, *The Great War in Modern Memory* (London: Oxford UP, 1975), 75.

66. Smith, *Frontier* 243–44.

67. Smith, *Frontier* 182.

68. Smith, *Frontier* 189.

69. Smith, *Novel* 215.

70. Smith, *Holiday* 10.

71. Smith, *Holiday* 95.

72. Virginia Woolf, *The Years* (New York: Harcourt, 1937).

73. Edward Said, *Orientalism* (New York: Vintage Books, 1978), 45.

74. Smith, *Holiday* 16.

75. Gilles Deleuze and Felix Guattari, *Anti-Oedipus: Capitalism and Schizophrenia,* trans. Robert Hurley, Mark Seem, and Helen R. Lane (Minneapolis: U of Minnesota P, 1983), 170.

76. Smith, *Holiday* 91.

77. Smith, *Holiday* 26–27.

78. Smith, *Holiday* 25.

79. Smith, *Holiday* 28.

80. Smith, *Holiday* 106.

81. Barbera and McBrien 167–68. Barbera and McBrien see the incestuous relationship between Caz and Celia as a representation of an androgyny. Although I agree, I think it is also important to see how the relationship between cousins challenges the romance plot and, therefore, the social order.

82. Smith, *Holiday* 143.

83. Smith, *Holiday* 140, 141.

84. Smith, *Holiday* 26.

85. Smith, *Holiday* 128.

86. Deleuze and Guattari 116.

87. Deleuze and Guattari 119.

88. Smith, *Holiday* 140.

89. Smith, *Holiday* 84.

CHAPTER 3. POEMS AND DRAWINGS: 1937–1966

1. Philip Larkin, "Frivolous and Vulnerable," in *In Search of Stevie Smith*, ed. Sanford Sternlicht (Syracuse, N.Y.: Syracuse UP, 1991), 77.

2. Jonathan Williams, "Much Further Out Than You Thought," in Sternlicht, *In Search of Stevie Smith* 47.

3. Jack Barbera and William McBrien, *Stevie: A Biography of Stevie Smith* (New York: Oxford UP, 1987), 192–94.

4. Barbera and McBrien 194–98.

5. Barbera and McBrien 199.

6. Barbera and McBrien 198.

7. See Romana Huk, "Eccentric Concentrism: Traditional Poetic Forms and

Refracted Discourse in Stevie Smith's Poetry," *Contemporary Literature* 34.2 (1993): 240–65, and Sheryl Stevenson, "Stevie Smith's Voices," *Contemporary Literature* 33 (1992): 24–45.

8. W. J. T. Mitchell, *Blake's Composite Art: A Study of the Illuminated Poetry* (Princeton, N.J.: Princeton UP, 1978), 3.

9. The early influence of Blake upon Smith is clear, as her copy of *The Poetical Works of William Blake* was bought in 1924. (See inscription in her copy at the University of Tulsa.) She also reviewed Blake's *Job* for both *Modern Woman* (December 1947) and the *Tribune* (26 December 1947). That Smith was familiar with Lear is clear from the fact that she reviewed *Nonsense Songs* (*Modern Woman*, March 1941; *Sunday Times*, 13 October 1968) and owned a copy of *A Nonsense Alphabet*, dated 1952 (copy at Tulsa); an early influence cannot be proved, though Smith's simple line drawings more clearly resemble Lear's than Blake's. Many critics also traced Smith's work to Blake and Lear: see Barbera and McBrien 101, 241, 299 (Blake), and 193, 241 (Lear); and Frances Spalding, *Stevie Smith: A Critical Biography* (London: Faber and Faber, 1988), 132, 269, 276 (Blake), and 259 (Lear).

10. Griselda Pollock, *Vision and Difference: Femininity, Feminism, and the Histories of Art* (London and New York: Routledge, 1988), 165.

11. Mitchell 23 (antipictorialism), 19 (symbolic vs. representational), 24 (emblems).

12. Barbera and McBrien 194.

13. Lisa Ede, "Edward Lear's Limericks and Their Illustrations," in *Explorations in the Field of Nonsense*, ed. Wim Tigges (Amsterdam: Rodopi, 1987), 104.

14. Barbera and McBrien 197–98.

15. Barbera and McBrien 199.

16. Craig Owens, "The Discourse of Others: Feminists and Postmodernism," in *The Anti-Aesthetic: Essays on Postmodern Culture*, ed. Hal Foster (Seattle, Wash.: Bay Press, 1983), 71.

17. Pollock 190. Pollock's book contains illustrations of Kelly's artwork.

18. Pollock 180.

19. Pollock 181.

20. Andreas Huyssen, *After the Great Divide: Modernism, Mass Culture, Postmodernism* (Bloomington: Indiana UP, 1986), 220–21.

21. Janice Winship, "A Woman's World: 'Woman'—an Ideology of Femininity," *Women Take Issue: Aspects of Women's Subordination* (Hutchinson: Women's Studies Group Centre for Contemporary Cultural Studies at the University of Birmingham, 1978), 140.

22. Stevie Smith, *Novel on Yellow Paper* (New York: Pinnacle Books, 1982), 132.

23. Martin Pugh, *Women and the Women's Movement in Britain, 1914–1959* (London: Macmillan, 1992), 83–87.

24. Dolores Hayden, *Redesigning the American Dream: The Future of Housing, Work, and Family Life* (New York: Norton, 1984), 75–76.

25. Hayden 77.

26. Pugh 87–90.

27. Sheila Jeffreys, *The Spinster and Her Enemies: Feminism and Sexuality, 1880–1930* (London: Pandora, 1985), 134.

28. Jeffreys 154.

29. Pugh 76; see also Billie Melman, *Women and the Popular Imagination in the Twenties* (New York: St. Martin's, 1988), 27–37.

30. Pugh 222.

31. Jeffreys 143–44.

32. Jeffreys 93–101, 128–46, 165–93.

33. Pugh 77; see also Melman 18, 20–21.

34. Melman 134–44.

35. W. J. T. Mitchell, *Iconology: Image, Text, Ideology* (Chicago and London: U of Chicago P, 1986), 43.

36. Mitchell, *Iconology* 95.

37. Hélène Cixous, "Sorties," in *New French Feminisms*, ed. Elaine Marks and Isabelle de Courtivron (New York: Schocken Books, 1981), 91.

38. Mitchell, *Iconology* 110.

39. Rachel Blau DuPlessis, *Writing beyond the Ending* (Bloomington: Indiana UP, 1985), 3–4.

40. DuPlessis 4.

41. Barbera and McBrien 198.

42. Stevie Smith, *Collected Poems* (New York: New Directions, 1983), 55.

43. Stevie Smith, "Dear Karl," *CP* 125. See reference to Whitman.

44. Smith, *CP* 117.

45. Christopher Ricks, "Stevie Smith: The Art of Sinking in Poetry," in Sternlicht, *In Search of Stevie Smith* 206.

46. Smith, *CP* 193.

47. Judy Little, "Endless Different Ways," in *Old Maids to Radical Spinsters*, ed. Laura Doan (Urbana: U of Illinois P, 1991), 30.

48. Smith, *CP* 298.

49. Stevie Smith, "My Muse," *Me Again: Uncollected Writings*, ed. Jack Barbera and William McBrien (New York: Vintage, 1983), 126.

50. Stevie Smith, "Lot's Wife," *CP* 210.

51. Smith, *CP* 179.

52. Barbera and McBrien 197.

53. Barbera and McBrien 198.

54. Stevie Smith, "Poems and Drawings III," BBC Third Programme, London, 21 July 1952. Script at BBC Written Archives.

55. Smith, *CP* 272.

56. Stevie Smith, "Too Tired for Words," BBC Third Programme, London, 4 March 1957. Script at University of Tulsa.

57. Smith, *CP* 21.

58. Mark Storey, "Why Stevie Smith Matters," in Sternlicht, *In Search of Stevie Smith* 191.

59. Smith, *CP* 425.

60. Janice Thaddeus, "Stevie Smith and the Gleeful Macabre," in Sternlicht, *In Search of Stevie Smith* 89.

61. Smith, *CP* 151.

62. Ann Colley, "Edward Lear's Limericks and the Reversals of Nonsense," *Victorian Poetry* 26.3 (Autumn 1988): 291.

63. Stevie Smith, *Harold's Leap* (London: Chapman and Hall, 1950), 22.

64. Huk 255.

65. Jack Barbera, "The Relevance of Stevie Smith's Drawings," *Journal of Modern Literature* 12 (July 1985): 233.

66. Smith, *CP* 303.

67. Thaddeus 95.

68. Stevie Smith, *Selected Poems* (New York: James Laughlin, 1964), 10.

69. Pollock 198.

70. Regina Barreca, *Untamed and Unabashed* (Detroit: Wayne State UP, 1994), 12.

71. Luce Irigaray, *Speculum of the Other Woman*, trans. Gillian C. Gill (Ithaca, N.Y.: Cornell UP, 1985), 142.

CHAPTER 4. THE BOOK REVIEWS: 1941–1951

1. Susan Sniader Lanser and Evelyn Torton Beck, "[Why] Are There No Great Women Critics?: And What Difference Does it Make?" *The Prism of Sex: Essays in the Sociology of Knowledge* (Madison: U of Wisconsin P, 1979), 79.

2. Lanser and Beck 79.

3. Lanser and Beck 84.

4. Lanser and Beck 84.

5. See the listing of Smith's reviews in Jack Barbera, William McBrien, and Helen Bajan's bibliography, *Stevie Smith: A Bibliography* (Westport, Conn.: Meckler, 1987), 6–77.

6. Jack Barbera and William McBrien, *Stevie: A Biography of Stevie Smith* (New York: Oxford UP, 1987), 90.

7. Barbera and McBrien 119.

8. Barbera and McBrien 135.

9. Frances Spalding, *Stevie Smith: A Critical Biography* (London: Faber and Faber, 1988), 169.

10. Spalding 169.

11. IIPA tables for 1939 listed in Pat Allatt, "The Family Seen through the Beveridge Report, Forces in Education and Popular Magazines. A Sociological Study of the Social Reproduction of Family Ideology in World War II," diss., University of Keele, 1981, 586–87.

12. Martin Pugh, *Women and the Women's Movement in Britain, 1914–1959* (London: Macmillan, 1992), 85.

13. Virginia Woolf, "The Common Reader," *The Common Reader* (London: Hogarth Press, 1951), 11–12.

14. Herbert Lindenberger, "Re-viewing the Reviews of *Historical Drama*," in *The Horizon of Literature*, ed. Paul Hernadi (Lincoln: U of Nebraska P, 1982), 283–85.

15. Lindenberger 285. See also Robert L. Patten's "Reviewing Reviewing: From

the Editor's Desk," in *Literary Reviewing,* ed. James O. Hoge (Charlottesville: UP of Virginia, 1987). Patten claims that he "can imagine circumstances in which [he] would commission any of them (reviewing styles)," but he inadvertently exposes his preference for the "all outer" and the "displacer," the most authoritarian forms, when he admires the "courage and conviction" (94) of the first, as well as the brilliant "ground razing" (93) of the second.

16. Stevie Smith, "Statement on Criticism," *Me Again: Uncollected Writings of Stevie Smith,* ed. Jack Barbera and William McBrien (New York: Vintage, 1983), 173.

17. Smith, "Statement on Criticism" 173.

18. Barbera and McBrien 170 (relationship with Holden), 113–15 (relationship with Lehmann), and 160 (review of Manning's *The Doves of Venus*); Spalding 211 (on Smith's generosity toward Holden and Dick).

19. Stevie Smith, "Stevie Smith Writes about Reading," *Modern Woman,* December 1946, 42.

20. Smith, "Reading" 42.

21. Smith, "Reading" 42.

22. Virginia Woolf, "Women and Fiction," *Collected Essays,* vol. 2 (New York: Harcourt Brace, 1967), 148.

23. Barbera and McBrien 224.

24. Stevie Smith, "History or Poetic Drama?" *Me Again* 152.

25. Diana Souhami, *A Woman's Place: The Changing Picture of Women in Britain* (Harmondsworth: Penguin Books, 1986), 46–47.

26. Pugh 264.

27. Pugh 265.

28. Gail Braybon and Penny Summerfield, *Out of the Cage: Women's Experiences in Two World Wars* (London: Pandora, 1987), 159.

29. Braybon and Summerfield 161.

30. Penny Summerfield, "'The girl that makes the thing that drills the hole that holds the spring . . .' Discourses of Women and Work in the Second World War," in *Nationalising Femininity: Culture, Sexuality, and British Cinema in the Second World War,* ed. C. Gledhill and G. Swanson, forthcoming from Manchester UP.

31. Summerfield.

32. It should be noted that this issue was published before women were required to register at their local Employment Exchange in March 1941.

33. Pugh 266–67.

34. Patricia Wentworth, "Torpedo," *Modern Woman,* February 1941, 52.

35. Beatrice Kane, "Why Year the Years," *Modern Woman,* February 1941, 36–38.

36. R. P., "Rock-A-Bye Baby!" *Modern Woman,* February 1941, 52.

37. Mary Gilbert, Home News Page, *Modern Woman,* February 1941, 33.

38. *Modern Woman,* February 1941, 3, 45.

39. *Modern Woman,* February 1941, 3, 46, 58.

40. "Just Talking," *Modern Woman,* February 1941, 5.

41. Joy Weston, "Money-Raiser," *Modern Woman,* February 1941, 16.

42. Braybon and Summerfield 279.

43. Janice Doane and Devon Hodges, *From Klein to Kristeva* (Ann Arbor: U of Michigan P, 1992), 24.

44. Braybon and Summerfield 280.

45. Judith Fetterley, *The Resisting Reader* (Bloomington: Indiana UP, 1981), xxii–xxiii.

46. Lindenberger 285. Patten too sees Lindenberger's scorn for the summary style (88–89).

47. Stevie Smith, "What Shall I Read?" *Modern Woman*, February 1941, 22.

48. Kate Flint, *The Woman Reader: 1837–1914* (Oxford: Clarendon Press, 1993), 241.

49. Stevie Smith, "Read and Relax," *Modern Woman*, September 1941, 18.

50. Stevie Smith, "New Books Reviewed by Stevie Smith," *Modern Woman*, November 1942, 40.

51. Stevie Smith, "Books," *Modern Woman*, August 1941, 20.

52. D. H. Lawrence, "Surgery for the Novel—or a Bomb," *Selected Literary Criticism* (New York: Viking Press, 1956), 118.

53. Stevie Smith, "Stevie Smith's Book Notes: Special for Christmas," *Modern Woman*, January 1949, 107.

54. Elizabeth Segel, "'As the Twig is Bent . . .': Gender and Childhood Reading," in *Gender and Reading: Essays on Readers, Texts, and Contexts*, ed. Elizabeth A. Flynn and Patrocino P. Schweickart (Baltimore: Johns Hopkins UP, 1986), 165.

55. Claudia Nelson, *Boys Will Be Girls* (New Brunswick and London: Rutgers UP, 1991); Flint.

56. Stevie Smith, "Heard of a Good Book?" *Modern Woman*, February 1942, 24.

57. Stevie Smith, "Heard of a Good Book?" *Modern Woman*, October 1942, 72.

58. Stevie Smith, "Buried in a Book," *Modern Woman*, October 1941, 38.

59. Stevie Smith, "I Do Like a Nice Book," *Modern Woman*, June 1941, 12.

60. Stevie Smith, "New Books Reviewed by Stevie Smith," *Modern Woman*, November 1942, 40.

61. Stevie Smith, "I Do Like a Nice Book," *Modern Woman*, May 1941, 22.

62. Stevie Smith, "Stevie Smith on 'Something to Read,'" *Modern Woman*, November 1941, 62; Stevie Smith, "For Your Book List," *Modern Woman*, April 1945, 35.

63. Stevie Smith, "What Shall I Read?" *Modern Woman*, April 1950, 78.

64. Stevie Smith, "A Book for the Beach," *Modern Woman*, June 1950, 89.

65. Stevie Smith, "Book Notes," *Modern Woman*, July 1947, 121.

CHAPTER 5. THE STORIES: 1939, 1946–1955

1. Elizabeth Wilson, *Only Halfway to Paradise* (London: Tavistock, 1980), 22.

2. Margaret D. Stetz, "*The Ghost and Mrs. Muir*: Laughing with the Captain in the House," *Studies in the Novel* 28.1 (Spring 1996): 96.

3. Martin Pugh, *Women and the Women's Movement in Britain, 1914–1959* (London: Macmillan, 1992), 286–87.

4. Alan Sinfield, *Literature, Politics, and Culture in Postwar Britain* (Berkeley and Los Angeles: U of California P, 1989), 205.

5. Wilson 71.

6. Wilson 16.

7. Wilson 43.

8. Sinfield 204.

9. Sinfield 205.

10. Sinfield 205.

11. Pugh 288.

12. Sinfield 210.

13. Sinfield 211.

14. Jack Barbera and William McBrien, *Stevie: A Biography of Stevie Smith* (New York: Oxford UP, 1987), 151.

15. Barbera and McBrien 185; Frances Spalding, *Stevie Smith: A Critical Biography* (London: Faber and Faber, 1988), 210, see also 189–90.

16. Niamh Baker, *Happily Ever After? Women's Fiction in Postwar Britain, 1945–1960* (New York: St. Martin's Press, 1989), 22.

17. Baker 21.

18. Stetz 94, 101.

19. Barbera and McBrien 75.

20. Frances Spalding (69, 111) refers to Parker only in relation to *Novel on Yellow Paper;* Barbera and McBrien (75) extend the Parker influence to Smith's letters.

21. Spalding 55.

22. Luce Irigaray, *Speculum of the Other Woman,* trans. Gillian C. Gill (Ithaca, N.Y.: Cornell UP, 1985), 142.

23. Based on catalogue of Smith's library, located at the McFarlin Library, University of Tulsa. All further references to Smith's collection are based on these data.

24. Three of Smith's works by Huxley, located at the University of Tulsa, are dated later than their original publication date: *Limbo* (1924), *Along the Road* (1930), and *Point Counterpoint* (1934). References to Smith's Huxley reviews may be found in Jack Barbera, William McBrien, and Helen Bajan, *Stevie Smith: A Bibliography* (Westport, Conn.: Meckler P, 1987), 14, 16, 19, 29, 44.

25. All four of Smith's works by Waugh, located at the University of Tulsa, are dated later, an indication that she found Waugh after Huxley: *When the Going Was Good* (1951), *A Handful of Dust* (1955), *Put Out More Flags* (1958), and *The Loved One* (1958). References to Smith's Waugh reviews: Barbera, McBrien, and Bajan 15, 20, 30, 45, 50, 58, 76.

26. Sandra Gilbert and Susan Gubar, *No Man's Land: The War of the Words* (New Haven and London: Yale UP, 1988), 132.

27. John Snyder, *Prospects of Power: Tragedy, Satire, the Essay, and the Theory of Genre* (Lexington: U of Kentucky P, 1991), 100.

28. Gilbert and Gubar 131–33.

29. Aldous Huxley, "Farcical History of Richard Greenow," *Limbo* (London: Chatto and Windus, 1920), 1–115.

30. Evelyn Waugh, *A Handful of Dust* (Boston: Little, Brown, 1934).
31. Nancy Walker, *A Very Serious Thing: Women's Humor and American Culture* (Minneapolis: U of Minnesota P, 1988), 13.
32. Walker 13.
33. Snyder 101.
34. Snyder 97.
35. Snyder 97.
36. Dorothy Parker, "Here We Are," *The Collected Stories of Dorothy Parker* (New York: Random House, 1942), 52.
37. Dorothy Parker, "Too Bad," *Collected Stories* 94.
38. Parker, "Too Bad" 99.
39. Anita Loos, *Gentlemen Prefer Blondes* and *But Gentlemen Marry Brunettes* (New York: Vintage, 1983), 161.
40. Stevie Smith, "The Herriots," *Me Again: Uncollected Writings of Stevie Smith,* ed. Jack Barbera and William McBrien (New York: Vintage, 1983), 78.
41. Stevie Smith, "Beside the Seaside," *Me Again* 15.
42. Stevie Smith, "Sunday at Home," *Me Again* 45.
43. Smith, "Sunday" 45.
44. Dorothy Parker, "Glory in Daytime," *Collected Stories* 302–3.
45. Dorothy Parker, "Mr. Durant," *Collected Stories* 119–120.
46. Loos, *Blondes* 26.
47. Stevie Smith, "A Very Pleasant Evening," *Me Again* 32–33.
48. Smith, "Seaside" 13.
49. Stevie Smith, "The Story of a Story," *Me Again* 50–59.
50. Dorothy Parker, "Big Blonde," *Collected Stories* 214.
51. Loos, *Blondes* 48.
52. Barbera and McBrien 65.
53. Smith, "Herriots" 76.
54. Snyder 134.
55. Stevie Smith, "Surrounded by Children," *Me Again* 26.
56. Mary Russo, "Female Grotesques: Carnival and Theory," in *Feminist Studies/Critical Studies,* ed. Teresa de Lauretis (Bloomington: Indiana UP, 1986), 214.
57. Russo 214.
58. Stevie Smith, "Getting Rid of Sadie," *Me Again* 39–43.
59. Jack Barbera, written comment to the author, 3 April 1995: "Surrounded by Children" acts as "Smith's nightmare of what life might be like if she were to remain unmarried—she might turn into a grotesque who remains a child."
60. Mikhail Bakhtin, *Rabelais and His World,* trans. Helene Iswolsky (Cambridge: M.I.T. Press, 1968), 11–12.
61. Smith, "Evening" 34.
62. Brian Attebery, *Strategies of Fantasy* (Bloomington: Indiana UP, 1992), 1.
63. Rachel Blau DuPlessis, *Writing beyond the Ending: Narrative Strategies of Twentieth-Century Women Writers* (Bloomington: Indiana UP, 1985), 179.
64. DuPlessis 179.
65. Smith, "Seaside" 22.
66. Smith uses this term, the "rhythm of friendship," in *Novel on Yellow*

Paper, but does not fully enact such a rhythm until *The Holiday.* Stevie Smith, *Novel on Yellow Paper* (New York: Pinnacle Books, 1982), 215.

67. Stevie Smith, "Is There a Life beyond the Gravy?" *Me Again* 73.

68. Smith, "Gravy" 63. See "The Magic Morning," where the girl who kills her boyfriend turns into a "slim stoat"; "My Hat," where the woman who flies away from society is compared to a swan; "The Wedding Photograph," where the young bride seems confident that she can lure a lion into killing her husband; "The Small Lady," where a woman turns into a duck upon escaping her home and washing machine; "Mrs. Blow and Her Animals," where Mrs. Blow dances with her animals and is taken care of by them. Stevie Smith, *Collected Poems* (New York: New Directions, 1983), 205–6, 315, 425, 471, 544–46.

69. Celia makes the connection between religion and school in *The Holiday* (New York: Pinnacle Books, 1982), 39–40.

70. Stevie Smith, "To School in Germany," *Me Again* 37.

71. Smith, *Holiday* 128.

72. Smith, "Sunday" 49.

73. Humbert Wolfe, *Notes on English Verse Satire* (New York: Harcourt, 1929), 7.

74. Spalding 168.

CHAPTER 6. THE SUNG POEMS: 1957–1971

1. Martin Pumphrey, "Play, Fantasy, and Strange Laughter: Stevie Smith's Uncomfortable Poetry," in *In Search of Stevie Smith,* ed. Sanford Sternlicht (Syracuse, N.Y.: Syracuse UP, 1991), 97–113.

2. See Sheryl Stevenson, "Stevie Smith's Voices," *Contemporary Literature* 33 (1992): 24–45, and Romana Huk, "Eccentric Concentrism: Traditional Poetic Forms and Refracted Discourse in Stevie Smith's Poetry," *Contemporary Literature* 34.2 (1993) 240–265. Stevenson opens her essay with a paragraph on Smith's performances, but shifts to a discussion of voice in her poetry.

3. One of Smith's staunchest supporters, Peter Dickinson, claims she is "not very musical" and "could not carry a tune," though adds, "that was part of her charm." Peter Dickinson, letters to the author, 19 August 1994 and 6 February 1996.

4. "Poetry and Sound," moderator George Macbeth, respondents Bob Cobbing, Kevin Koster Holland, Alan Little, Eric Mottram, Peter Porter, and Tim Sister, recorded 18 June 1966, Royal Albert Hall, broadcast 16 February 1968, 20:45, Radio 3 Third Programme. Available at National Sound Archive, London.

5. Seamus Heaney, "A Memorable Voice: Stevie Smith," in Sternlicht, *In Search of Stevie Smith* 211.

6. Judith Butler, *Gender Trouble: Feminism and the Subversion of Identity* (New York and London: Routledge, 1990), 138.

7. Peggy Phelan, *Unmarked: The Politics of Performance* (New York and London: Routledge, 1993), 164.

8. Frances Spalding, *Stevie Smith: A Critical Biography* (London: Faber and Faber, 1988), 203–4.

9. *Oxford English Dictionary,* S.V. "revue"; Lois Rutherford, " 'Harmless Nonsense': The Comic Sketch and the Development of Music-Hall Entertainment, in *Music Hall: Performance and Style,* ed. J. S. Bratton (Milton Keynes: Open UP, 1986), 132.

10. "Glenda Jackson Reads Stevie Smith," Argo ZSW 608. Available at the National Sound Archive, London.

11. Jack Barbera, William McBrien, and Helen Bajan list her recordings in their bibliography, *Stevie Smith: A Bibliography* (Westport, Conn.: Meckler, 1987), 108–16. See also Peter Dickinson, *Stevie's Tunes* (London: Novello, 1988).

12. Kate Whitehead, *The Third Programme: A Literary History* (Oxford: Clarendon Press, 1989), 9.

13. Whitehead 52.

14. Whitehead 18.

15. Spalding 231.

16. Spalding 204–7, 230–33; Jack Barbera and William McBrien, *Stevie: A Biography of Stevie Smith* (New York: Oxford UP, 1987), 184.

17. Spalding 204–7; Barbera and McBrien 184. Barbera and McBrien mention that Smith intended her fourth poetry program to include settings of her poems.

18. Spalding 230–33.

19. Spalding 232, 233.

20. Spalding 263, 264.

21. Spalding 268.

22. Spalding 269.

23. Anthony Bennett, "Music in the Halls," in *Music Hall: Performance and Style,* ed. J. S. Bratton (Milton Keynes: Open UP, 1986), 2–6.

24. J. S. Bratton, Introduction, *Music Hall* x.

25. Bratton xi.

26. Dave Russell, *Popular Music in England, 1840–1914* (Kingston and Montreal: McGill-Queen's UP, 1987), 97.

27. Russell 97.

28. Bratton, Introduction xiv.

29. Martha Vicinus, *The Industrial Muse* (New York: Barnes and Noble, 1974), 265.

30. J. S. Bratton, "Jenny Hill: Sex and Sexism in the Victorian Music Hall," in Bratton, *Music Hall* 105–6.

31. Henry M. Sayre, *The Object of Performance* (Chicago: U of Chicago P, 1989), 7.

32. Cary Nelson, *Repression and Recovery: Modern American Poetry and the Politics of Cultural Memory, 1910–1945* (Madison: U of Wisconsin P, 1989), 61.

33. There are, of course, many renditions of "The Coventry Carol"; see Robert Croo, "The Coventry Carol," *Oxford Book of Carols* (Oxford: Oxford UP, 1941), 46–47.

34. Stevie Smith, "To the Tune of the Coventry Carol," *Collected Poems* (New York: New Directions, 1983), 25.

35. Gerrard Williams, arr., "Golden Slumbers," in *Daily Express Community*

Song Book, ed. John Goss (London: Daily Express National Community Singing Movement, 1927), 73.

36. Stevie Smith, "The Devil-my-Wife," *CP,* 198.

37. Dickinson 14–16.

38. Stevie Smith, "The Warden," *Stevie Smith Reads Selected Poems,* recorded 30 July 1965, Marvel Press Listen LPV7; "The Warden," "People in Rather Odd Circumstances: The Poems, Drawings and Conversation of Stevie Smith," Monitor No. 148, broadcast 6 April 1965, 22:34, BBC1, NSA T7364 W. Available at National Sound Archive, London.

39. Jane Traies, "Jones and the Working Girl: Class Marginality in Music-Hall Song, 1860–1900," in Bratton, *Music Hall,* 44.

40. Fred E. Weatherly (lyrics), "The Children's Home," London: Morley Jr. and Co., 189–.

41. Stevie Smith, "The Warden," *CP* 232.

42. Stevie Smith, "Silence and Tears," *Stevie Smith Reads Selected Poems,* recorded 30 July 1965, Marvel Press Listen LPV7. Available at National Sound Archive, London.

43. Stevie Smith, "Silence and Tears," *CP* 110.

44. Tina Darragh, letter to the author, 5 September 1993.

45. Stevie Smith, "Le Désert de l'Amour," "Contemporary Poets Reading Their Own Poems," recorded 31 December 1968, NSA 1819 B, BC 1514. Available at National Sound Archive, London.

46. Stevie Smith, "Le Désert de l'Amour," *Collected Poems* (New York: New Directions, 1983) 120.

47. Stevie Smith, "The Repentance of Lady T," "Poets in Public," recorded in the Freemasons' Hall during the Edinburgh Festival, broadcast live 27 Aug. 1965, 21:00, Third Programme, NSA 5667W, BBC MT. Available at National Sound Archive, London.

48. Stevie Smith, "The Repentance of Lady T," *CP* 199.

49. Stevie Smith, "Do Take Muriel Out," "Poets in Public," recorded in the Freemasons' Hall during the Edinburgh Festival, broadcast live 27 August 1965, 21:00, Third Programme, NSA 5667W, BBC MT 31598; also, "New Moon Carnival," recorded 18 June 1966, Royal Albert Hall, broadcast 19 July 1966, 19:30, Third Programme, NSA C 162/8. Available at National Sound Archive, London.

50. Stevie Smith, "Do Take Muriel Out," *CP* 250.

51. "Stevie Smith," "Poems and Drawings by Stevie Smith I," transmission 28 March 1951, recorded 21 February 1951. Script available at BBC Written Archives Centre, Reading.

52. "Poetry and Sound."

53. Stevie Smith, "The Heavenly City," *CP,* 193.

54. St. Bernard of Clairvaux and Alexander Ewing, "Jerusalem the Golden," in *Songs That Changed the World,* ed. Wanda Willson Whitman (New York: Crown, 1969), 105.

55. Stevie Smith, "'Oh stubborn race of Cadmus' Seed . . . ,'" *Stevie Smith Reads Selected Poems,* recorded 30 July 1965, Marvel Press Listen LPV7. Available at National Sound Archive, London.

56. Stevie Smith, "Poems and Drawings III," transmission 21 July 1952, recorded 28 May 1952. Available at BBC Written Archives Centre, Reading.

57. "Poems and Drawings III." Available at BBC Written Archives Centre, Reading.

58. Stevie Smith, "One of Many," "Poets in Public," recorded in Freemasons' Hall during the Edinburgh Festival, broadcast live 27 August 1965, 21:00, Third Programme, NSA 884 R, BBC T 31642. Available at National Sound Archive, London.

59. Stevie Smith, "One of Many," *CP* 101. In a c. 1945 letter to Kay Dick, Smith refers to the poem as a self-portrait: Stevie Smith, *Me Again: Uncollected Writings of Stevie Smith*, ed. Jack Barbera and William McBrien (New York: Vintage, 1983), 288.

60. Spalding 270.

61. Bratton, Introduction xi.

62. Thomas Leitch, "Passivity Squared Equals Activism: An Alternative to the Myth of the Inscribed Audience," in *Styles of Cultural Activism,* ed. Philip Goldstein (Newark: U of Delaware P, 1994), 92.

63. Deposited, along with the rest of Stevie Smith's books, in the McFarlin library at the University of Tulsa.

Index

159

Index

Parker, Dorothy, 18, 22, 25, 98, 99, 101, 102–9, 110, 116
Payn, James, 25–27
Pearson's, 3, 8–13, 53. *See also* Newnes, Pearson
Pearson's Magazine, 8, 9, 10, 12–13
Peg's Paper, 8, 9, 11, 12, 13, 25
Proust, Marcel, 28

Rathbone, Eleanor, 5, 7
Rhondda, Viscountess (Margaret Haig), 5
Richardson, Dorothy, 18, 21, 25, 28, 30, 31, 41
Royal, The, 8, 9, 13
Royden, Maude, 5

Smallwood, Norah, 4
Smith, Stevie
  and BBC, the, 119–22
  and colonialism, 42–47, 54–55, 64, 68, 69, 71
  and consumerism, 15–16
  and domestic ideology, 13–16, 16–18, 23, 25–26, 28–30, 35–36, 54–57, 58, 74, 77–78, 81, 87, 88, 90–91, 92, 101–2, 108–9, 110, 125–26, 128, 131, 133
  and fantasy, 101–2, 111–15
  and feminism, 5–7, 18–19, 23, 31, 32, 42, 49, 51–53, 74–75, 77–78, 95, 98, 99, 101, 108–9, 118, 125, 138
  and modernism, 16–17, 24–25, 74, 86, 90. *See* additional entries under Eliot, Richardson, Stein, and Woolf.
  and music hall, 18, 22, 117, 119, 122–25, 128, 138
  and nature, depiction of, 32, 34, 57–58, 61–63, 64, 68
  and New Woman novelists, 31, 98
  and performance, 18, 21, 118, 127–33, 133–38
  and postmodernism, 20–21, 23, 50, 88
  and postwar women fiction writers, 98
  and superfluous women, 49, 54–55, 56–57, 70–74
  and Victorian novelists, 25–27
  and violence against women, 58–59, 64, 69, 111, 113–14
  and women's magazines, 13–16, 53, 78, 80–81, 87–95

  and women's reading, 16–17, 78, 80–81, 87–95
  and women's satire, 98–99, 100–102, 102–9, 109–16
  —Broadcasts (Recorded)
  "Contemporary Poets Reading Their Own Poems" (recorded Dec. 31, 1968): "Le Désert de l'Amour," 131–32
  "New Moon Carnival" (recorded June 18, 1966): "Do Take Muriel Out," 135–36
  "People in Rather Odd Circumstances: The Poems, Drawings and Conversation of Stevie Smith" (recorded Apr. 6, 1965): "The Warden," 128–29
  "Poems by Stevie Smith" (recorded Mar. 28, 1956), 121
  "Poets in Pubic"/Edinburgh Festival Reading (broadcast live Aug. 27, 1965): "Do Take Muriel Out," 135; "One of Many," 137; "The Repentance of Lady T," 134–35
  —Broadcasts (Scripts)
  "A Turn Outside," 121
  "Poems and Drawings I" (recorded 21 Feb., 1951), 121, 135
  "Poems and Drawings III" (recorded 28 May, 1952), 65, 121, 137
  "Too Tired for Words," 121
  —Commercial Recording
  Stevie Smith Reads Selected Poems (Marvel Press Listen): "'Oh stubborn race of Cadums' Seed . . .'," 137; "Silence and Tears," 129–31; "The Warden," 128–29
  —Essays
  "History or Poetic Drama?," 5, 17, 81–82
  "My Muse," 63
  "Statement on Criticism," 79–80
  "Stevie Smith Writes about Reading" (*MW* Dec. 1946), 81
  "Syler's Green," 121
  —Novels
  Novel on Yellow Paper, 4, 5, 8, 12, 13, 15, 16, 17, 18, 24, 25, 27, 28, 29, 30–36, 39, 42, 53, 77, 99
  Over the Frontier, 6, 24, 30, 36–42
  The Holiday, 6, 17, 24, 28, 30, 41, 42–47, 102, 112–14

160

Index

Tennyson, Alfred, 6, 18
Tilley, Vesta, 123
Turner, Joseph Mallord William, 51,
    61–62, 63

Victoria, Vesta, 123

Ward, Mrs. Humphry, 25–27, 29, 35–36
Waugh, Evelyn, 22, 48, 99–100, 101, 115

West, Rebecca, 6
Whitman, Walt, 58, 63
Woolf, Virginia: general, 18, 21, 25, 28,
    31, 32, 37, 76; *A Room of One's Own,*
    34; "The Common Reader," 78; *The*
    Years, 29, 30, 42, 43, 44; *Three Guineas,*
    14, 27, 29, 39–40, 41, 42; "Women and
    Fiction," 81

162